DISCOVERY

OF

LESS

First published by Less is Progress Limited, 2021

Copyright © Chris Lovett, 2021

The moral rights of the author have been asserted.

A CIP catalogue record for this book is available from the British Library

Cover design and interiors by Matt Windsor (thedesigngarden.co.uk)

All enquiries to info@lessisprogress.com

ISBN: 978-1-8384375-0-3

Printed by Ingram Spark

www.lessisprogress.com

10 9 8 7 6 5 4 3 2 1

Chris Lovett

DISCOVERY

OF

LESS

How I Found Everything I Wanted
Underneath Everything I Owned

Praise for *Discovery of Less*

"Chris Lovett offers a remarkably insightful look into what one can accomplish by disrupting our view of more, and the discovery of less. Bravo!"
Whitney Johnson, award-winning author of *Disrupt Yourself* and *Thinkers50 Leading Management Thinkers*

"Like a dip in an icy lake, this book allows you to feel alive again. Inspiring yet practical, it's a compelling argument to assess life in the context of getting more, by adopting a philosophy of 'simple and less'. A great contribution to the area of personal improvement."
Jamil Qureshi, Performance Coach and Psychologist

"I was pleasantly surprised how much I enjoyed reading Chris Lovett's personal journey towards owning less stuff. I found his style of writing with candor and humor refreshing. His stories illuminate the absurdity of keeping large quantities of things that aren't being used or enjoyed. Discovery of Less rises to the challenge of adding value and a fresh voice to the movement of minimalism."
Lisa J. Shultz, author of *Lighter Living*

"Chris has inspired me to take the plunge. Taking my foot off the materialist pedal makes perfect happiness sense!"
Dr Andy Cope, Dr of Happiness and bestselling author of *How to be a Well Being*

"This book will inspire more people to simplify and take back control of their lives."
Andy Storch, Author of *Own Your Career Own Your Life* and host of *Talent Development Hot Seat* podcast

"*Chris Lovett brings light and humor to an often dark and cold space of minimalism. Read his story to let go of more, and to reach your potential.*"
Justin Malik, Host/Producer, *Optimal Living Daily* podcast

"*Chris Lovett has articulated something that feels timely and important. I was immediately struck by the resonance of the idea then immediately inspired to respond.*"
Bruce Daisley, Bestselling author of *The Joy of Work* and host of Apple #1 business podcast *Eat, Sleep, Work, Repeat*

"*Chris is a text-book example of the positive, enriching outcomes of decluttering. We literally feel his shoulders lower and settle as he takes us through his journey towards minimalism. Here's to him inspiring his readers to give themselves permission to crack on with their own decluttering journeys, boost their wellbeing and make their own discoveries.*"
Caroline Rogers, Author of "Home and the Extended-Self: The Association Between Clutter and Wellbeing", *Journal of Environmental Psychology*, 2021

"*Chris brings a freshness, honesty and humour to the world of minimalism and intentional living in Discovery of Less. His storytelling captured my heart and mind. Whether you're a hardcore minimalist or this is the first book you ever pick up on minimalism, you'll laugh, be inspired and ultimately walk away determined to live with less.*"
Amy Revell, Host of *The Art of Decluttering* podcast and author of *Simply Organised*

About the Author

Chris Lovett is a minimalist, author, speaker, career mentor, professional executive coach and simplicity coach. Through his talks, blogs and seminars he unlocks the potential of individuals, families, teams and organisations through *doing less*. His words have touched thousands of lives in more than forty-five countries, inspiring and empowering people to let go of material possessions and unlocking their potential by removing the stuff that gets in the way. He has been featured prominently on platforms such as No Sidebar, Minimalism Life and Optimal Living Daily and has talked at festivals, well-being events, financial institutions and consultancy firms across the UK.

Discover more online at lessisprogress.com

Contents

Discovery Begins Now

*"Never underestimate the importance of abandoning crap you don't need.
It has the power to change your life."*
Joshua Becker,
Forbes.com, 2018

Let's go...

Most of us have too much clutter. We may not be fully aware of it yet but it's there. And by clutter, I mean anything physical, digital, mental or emotional that gets in the way of achieving our goals and living a fulfilling life.

Either consciously or subconsciously, we've all decided to surround ourselves with stuff that doesn't benefit us or enhance our life experience, and yet we leave it in our immediate environments to take up room – physical and psychological – in our lives. Most of us live with an abundance of crap locked away in cupboards, in the back of wardrobes, up lofts, down basements, in garages or out at storage units that we pay additional rent for.

The work-life calendar always looks stacked and we've all made the choice, somewhere down the line, to determine that 'busy' just doesn't cut it anymore so we proclaim to be 'super-busy', anything to foster the appearance of "If we're super-busy, we must have significance, *purpose.*"

It's a lie.

Our handheld 'smart' devices are littered with pointless email subscriptions that add no value, 'friends' who aren't friends at all, unused networking connections, useless old contacts and random stuff like that car parking app you used that one time, five years ago. Feel free to take a second and delete it now, if you like. Happy to wait.

Excuses, comparisons and mistruths spam our minds, polluting them with self-inflicted limitations. The stories we tell ourselves hold us back from letting go and progressing. Previous ambitions and aspirations are left as "what ifs", dreams or fantasies destined to remain unfulfilled. What we might be dealing with now is that the stuff we decided to bring into our lives to take ownership of, now actually owns us.

Of course, I am not the first to say this. Nor will I be the last. But I am here to tell you what you already know: it has to stop.

The clothes that no longer fit, the DVDs we've never watched and the instruction manuals to electronics we no longer own remain in our close proximities, surrounding us, suffocating us, defeating us. Why? Because we – me, you, all of us – find it incredibly difficult to let go of stuff. The useless shit we've surrounded ourselves with is holding us back from moving forward. It's keeping us tethered to the ground, an anchor dragging us down, keeping us in the same spot. It's getting in the way of us taking control of our lives. It's keeping us restrained to the decisions of the past. It's blocking our growth. It's stopping us from unlocking our potential.

And this applies to everyone. You're not alone.

Today, as I write this at the end of 2020, a year that has taken the entire world by surprise, a year that has become referred to as the "global reset button", a chance has appeared. Residents of Planet Earth have, in a lot of cases I have observed, had the opportunity to take stock of what matters in their lives. Much of the world has been stuck indoors on lockdown, in isolation, quarantined, furloughed, bored. Those people have had the chance to look around their living spaces and realise what is important to them. And, most importantly, what is not. Time has slowed, and, in some instances, it's revealed an opportunity to stop the clock and then throw it out. The movement towards less is growing with each new day, and the COVID-19 pandemic has accelerated that movement forward. *The Washington Post* recently coined the line 'The Great Decluttering of 2020' following a wave of Americans cleaning out their homes mid-pandemic. A lot of us have also been forced to turn previously unused pockets of our homes into workspaces, shifting stuff and things around to make room for a home office set-up. The body of evidence is growing that clutter in all its shapeshifting forms negatively impacts our well-being and ability to achieve the things we want to.

In 2019, following a study of 2,000 Brits, commissioned by the online lender MyJar, it was estimated that Britain's material clutter alone was worth up to £81.6 billion. That's not a typo, that's BILLION!

A survey done prior to Fashion Week 2018 by a large

shopping centre in Fleetwood showed that 72 per cent of shoppers admitted to having completely unworn clothing in their wardrobe, with a further 51 per cent confessing to being aware they would probably never wear the item when they actually bought it. That's just one survey, one data source, out of scores available online.

Recently, eBay revealed that a typical UK household could be stashing "thousands of pounds" worth of unused gear in the dark corners of their home.

And the stats continue to stack up:

- The National Association of Professional Organisers in the US reports that one in eleven American households spend over $1,000 a year hiring additional storage space.
- The average ten-year-old owns 238 toys but only plays with twelve daily according to a report in the *Telegraph*.
- A recent study by Princeton University found clutter to decrease productivity. This is important because the university felt compelled to do the study in the first place.
- Research conducted by comparethemarket.com revealed that the UK hoards more clutter than the rest of Europe. Go UK!
- Cornell University experimented with cluttered and chaotic environments and found a link between a disorganised, messy environment and poor eating choices. Clutter makes us fucking fat now. Wonderful.
- 54 per cent of Americans are overwhelmed by the amount of clutter they have, but 78 per cent of those have no idea what to do with it.
- Clutter can make us feel stressed, anxious and depressed according to scientists from the University of California. They found that the levels of the stress hormone cortisol were higher in mothers whose home environment was cluttered.
- UK employees ranked meaningless tasks as their number one factor keeping them from feeling fulfilled at work. The

2020 state of work report published by Workfront also mentioned that the majority (60 per cent) of an employee's day is wasted on excessive emails, unproductive meetings and a lack of standard processes and collaboration.

- Mental clutter is thought to be one of the prime suspects in the cause of age-related memory loss. The University of Toronto's Lynn Hasher proposed this a number of years ago and her research continues to support that proposition. Shit.

· · · · · ⓢ · · · · · ·

In the time it took to read the facts and statistics above, you no doubt received an email telling you about a discount you have no interest in from a business you haven't bought anything from in years. Feel free to take a moment and unsubscribe from that mailing list. Trust me, it'll feel good.

Our digital clutter constantly wrestles our attention away from the thing our minds are meant to be focused on. The pings and bleeps on our phones and laptops distract us from being creative and getting into a flow state, that sense of fluidity between body and mind where you are totally absorbed in something beyond the point of distraction.

I could go on, but you get the picture. All this stuff we've brought into our homes, our safe spaces that we've invested so much in, holds us back from being the version of ourselves we have always aspired to be. How many times have we said, "I'd love to do _____ *but I just don't have the time.*"?

But there is hope. Some of us are slowly waking from our stuff-induced slumber and becoming more aware of the impact pointless material possessions have on our behaviours, health and pockets, and the positive thing here is that it all starts with you, your habits and your stuff.

It's time to cut the crap, basically. The clutter in your home is like junk food – absolutely brilliant when you gorge on it, but of no nutritional value later on, and potentially harmful to your health.

You know when something is becoming more important when you see it become an awareness week. One for your calendar – Clutter Awareness Week in the US started in 2018 and runs every third week in March. Plus of course we have the annual Spring-cleaning tradition that dates back through religions and cultures to at least the 1800s. National Hoarding Awareness Week runs each May for those of us in the UK, by the way.

Up until 2016, I thought no differently than anyone else. Life, my home, my body, my work – it was all about how much stuff I could consume or do. I was quite complacent, drifting through life with stale routine and regularity. I was collecting all sorts of stuff, like excessive amounts of clothes and entertainment. Not exactly the stuff I wanted to collect, but stuff none the less. I had a whole bunch of aspirations such as learning to play the guitar but my collection of things mixed with an excessive To-Do list, self-sabotaging thoughts and a lack of awareness of my values and capabilities all just made me feel like I'd created a load of limitations, a self-made ceiling, a prison so to speak, and I was the primary inmate. My prison walls included credit card debt, fast fashion, negative self-fulfilling prophecies such as expecting things to go wrong and telling myself I was never good enough, a risk-averse outlook on life, an unfulfilling career, irrational comparisons to successful people, tons of unused 'just in case' items around the home, like spare tools and fancy kitchen utensils, and a fixed mindset that kept me at just the right level of safe, slap bang in the middle of a rather large comfort zone. I lived month to month with the salary I earned for a thirty-five-hour working week, but I wasn't really living at all. Existing, mainly, going from A to Z, without thinking of the letters in-between. Part of my journey since then has been to climb my way out of the place of confinement I was clinging to and then just learning how to... *let go*.

The clutter I had accumulated since I was a teenager

(excluding all my toys and football memorabilia in my parents' loft that they had kept – more of which later) became a picture of my jumbled, busy life lacking direction, and by letting go of it, piece by piece, item by item, day by day, I started to create a new path to make room to do the things I really wanted to do. To live a life more fulfilled. A life less ordinary.

One of the extraordinary things I set my mind on was to travel. Not an extended holiday.

Travel. See the world.

But in order to do that, I first had to hit the reset button on my life.

I sold, donated, recycled and discarded everything that no longer added value to my life. I pivoted my career to something much more meaningful, something for me, and replaced the mental clutter and stories I had hoarded for so many years with new knowledge and experiences. It wasn't easy, and it wasn't an overnight success. It took time, commitment and the ability to look at my old life and admit what was going wrong, where I was wasting my potential. Letting go of the identity I had forged with all my purchasing habits and possessions was, at first, a struggle. Coming to terms with deliberately walking away from habits, routines, thoughts and the security of a job, a home and a traditional approach to life was quite a task. It took a lot of soul searching (whatever that means) to work out what I wanted to do and how I wanted to show up for the rest of my life. No easy thing. Try it.

As all this stuff was carefully extracted out of my "mental desktop" (as I call it), I started to curate a new lifestyle and develop a new mindset. With those new experiences of travelling, pivoting careers (twice) and being more thoughtful of where I was spending my resources, came an increased level of growth and realisation: I could achieve so much more and live quite happily with so much less. In fact, I coined a term, a motto, mantra that I now live by…

LESS IS PROGRESS.

I now layer a bespoke minimalist lifestyle across all areas

of my life from my home, to my career, to my hobbies, my relationships and my day-to-day decisions. I routinely say to myself, "Is this thing adding value?" And if the answer is no, you know where it goes.

Once I developed, and trained, this minimalist mindset – and, again, it took time, patience and dedication – I continued to spend thousands of hours listening, reading, researching and absorbing all the variations and intricacies of minimalism, essentialism and simple living from those who went before me and showed the way: Joshua Becker, Fumio Sasaki, Courtney Carver, The Minimalists, Greg McKeown, and many other guiding lights from around the globe. Collectively, they all questioned the same ideas without trying to find some pretentious or overbearing answer: just a simpler way to live better.

In doing so, a general theme started to appear. What I discovered, including in my own experience, was that people tended to have to experience trauma, a bad decision or a series of negative events before then realising what was important. Whether it be a death in the family, missing an important event for the sake of something less important, recovering from addiction, or a physical or mental health issue, the theme is that when bad things happen, we wake up and decide to make changes. Well, guess what, you don't have to wait to experience a trauma before beginning to let go of the things that don't enhance your life. You can start anytime, and I think most of us have been presented with some kind of crossroads recently.

After my own reawakening (my "conscious uncoupling" from my old life; it was indeed a "Eureka!" moment), and armed with a broader view of the minimalist lifestyle, I began conducting my life with decluttering at the heart of every decision: I began appearing on minimalism podcasts and speaking at well-being and business events, re-telling a shorter version of my story that you are about to read. I observed one thing: People were fascinated with my journey. They would lean forward in their chairs, interrupt with questions and then tell me their own collection of stuff they'd been carrying around for years. My story resonated with them, because either they had personal crap they had held on to or they knew someone who did. One person even recommended writing a book. I laughed it off. But as time went on, even more similar comments started to land and there's only so many times you can hear, "You should write a book about this," before you then start to take it seriously.

So, what you will find in this book is a collection of stories over a period of four-or-so years. In this time, I realised two things: one, my stuff owned me, and two, what I was able to achieve once I got rid of it. There is no one-size-fits-all approach to letting go of your stuff – I use the word collectively to mean anything physical, emotional, digital or mental you own that you don't need to – but there are common thoughts that make the whole thing more difficult that we would initially think. But minimalism and having a minimalist mindset doesn't have to be this big weighty topic that is always super-serious and poignant. The ability to look at our past habits and learn from them in a fun way can make it easier to focus forwards and, actually, enjoy the process. Indeed, science tells us that decluttering is a positive first step to non-religious illumination. Let's have a laugh with it, shall we?

What you won't find in the following pages is a load of bull-shit must-do demands from up on high. I'm not that guy. Giving advice is natural to all of us and it makes us feel better, however I believe that most people who want to make this change in their life are intelligent and resourceful enough to take new information and formulate it to how it will work in their own unique situation. Letting go is not something you have to take verbatim from someone else, it's adapting it for your own requirements.

Since my Big Reset, I've spoken at public and private events all over London, Birmingham, Edinburgh, and then dozens of times from the comfort of my living room (and once in the bedroom) virtually during COVID-19. Those seminars have helped many corporate teams simplify their work and decompress from the excessive To-Do lists, and I've seen the light bulb go on for people. In fact, 96 percent of people in a recent survey by Azlo, a banking platform for small business owners, said that the pandemic actually motivated them to finally start their own business. I've coached and mentored clients of all shapes and sizes through their own decluttering journey – or declut, as I have abridged it, in a stupid attempt to waste even less mental CPU – whether it be the material possessions in their home, no longer being hostage to emotional baggage, letting go of self-sabotaging stories or replacing a job they hate with one they love. Or, at the very least, one they can tolerate. I've talked my way onto various podcasts and my words have featured in several "simple living" blogs such as Minimalism Life and No Sidebar. These blogs, as well as the podcasts, and social influencers, are enjoying more critical and commercial success with each passing day. And while "simple living" may feel "on trend" right now, the truth is it has always been under people's noses, and it always will be spring cleaning remember, but there is something in the water, in 2020 and beyond, that has accelerated its popularity. Research by McKinsey & Company between mid-March and early April 2020 found that Americans planned to spend 50 per cent less than usual on clothing and electronics over the following few weeks. And, you know what, people consuming less and spending more time on what's important is a good thing, no matter how anyone spins it.

As I always tell my fellow aspiring minimalists online or at events, everything you are about to read in this book is 100 per cent true. None of it has been dramatised or embellished for your entertainment. Some names may have changed but that's about it.

As you slowly breeze through my timeline, you'll be able to see the signs. Those discreet moments of indecision, busyness and self-created obstacles, along with all the clutter that was getting in the way, that made my life require a rethink. When you take your journey, you'll also pick up on your own signs. Picking up this book could be the first. Take the time to pause when something resonates and think about whether those similar things that you have in your environment really amplify your experience of life or if you'd prefer to be spending your resources (time, money, energy) on something more interesting. I wrote this because I was stuck and think it's an important journey to share. If you are in some way consumed by stuff or just feeling stuck in life, this is for you. I hope some of the stories within help you to unlock your potential as they did mine. And if they do, tell your stories to others, as I have done. The more we all talk positively about our shared experiences, the more we all live better, healthier and more productive lives. And isn't that something to celebrate – certainly as the world order seems more unstable than ever.

So, yes, now I define myself as a minimalist, a simplicity, career and exec coach, a mentor, speaker, writer, thought leader, storyteller and, most importantly, doggie parent. Not labels I would have ever in my wildest dreams thought I would collect but to be honest, it's a collection I much prefer.

I am more with less. You can be too…

PHASE ONE

Lots To Do

"I'd like to find out why I'm so busy, but I just can't find the time to do it."
Everyone

1. Breaking Point

I didn't sleep particularly well last night. It was one of those sleeps where you have to wake up earlier than usual, but you don't fully trust that you've set the alarm right. Two mini-panics checking the clock throughout the night have disturbed my few hours of hibernation preparing for the big day today. I've booked a meeting with my boss, Amanda, about my recent request for a sabbatical to take some time away from work – catching bad guys from behind a desk. That's what I told strangers at parties, anyway. Sounds a lot cooler than it was, not that the job itself was bad, it wasn't. It was just bad for me. It involved a lot of analysis of systems, drinking copious amounts of water and attending mind-numbing meetings. You know, the usual nine-to-five stuff.

My "day job" was something I fumbled into really, as I'm sure most corporate workers will say. What was once a job that simply paid for my extensive high-street and online shopping habits and boozy weekend nights out had now turned into a career.

I always wanted to be a footballer or be in a band, but I've just ended up sitting on my arse all day.

So, what did I do, I hear you ask?

I was responsible for leading a team of crime analysts in a medium-sized insurance company with the aim of protecting it and the public from falling foul of scams. The company tried to understand the latest trends that impacted society in order to figure out how people could avoid becoming a victim or even accidently facilitate the laundering of dirty money from another crime. Every now and then I would collaborate with the police to collar serial offenders, which sometimes led to the disruption of illegal activity or a juicy fine. Sometimes, the fraudsters out-smarted our triggers and we would lose a load of money to organised and opportunistic bad guys who would circumnavigate the company's systems and take advantage of vulnerable customers or ill-informed staff. It sounded exciting, and in fairness it used to be. On the face of it, I was actually quite comfortable at work.

It had the somewhat interesting subject matter of stopping low-level crime and protecting the public. However, over the course of a few years, I started to become a bit bored and wondered if this was it for me, a stable life of mediocrity.

A request to take a career break was not as common or as easy as people might have thought, and although it was generally seen as a good thing, it left a trail of holes to fill. My manager, Amanda, wanted to have a chat with me in person before making it official. I told her in January 2017 that I intended to take ten months off, starting August 2017. Telling her then gave her eight months' notice, which was the least I could do. Probably not a meeting she expected to have at the start of a new year but why not start it with a bang, right?

Ten months seemed like a solid round number, one month for each year I'd worked there. Due to my unbroken length of service, I qualified for a sabbatical, an employee 'perk' I never thought I'd actually use.

I had booked myself on the earliest train from London to Bournemouth, which is where Amanda was based and where the company's headquarters were. The office was situated on a busy roundabout in the middle of town a few miles away from the famed stretch of Britain's goldenest sands. It's a trip I'd done so many times over the years that I knew all the stops, the best place on the train to sit, what carriage was closest to the station exit and where precisely the 4G would drop out. Once on the train, it was a journey I actually enjoyed. I could sit and relax for a couple of hours, listening to music as the train meandered through the New Forest National Park. Sometimes I even treated myself to a little unplanned snooze.

Before the journey, however, I had to first hoist myself out of deep golden slumber. Those last few magical moments in bed were coming to an end as the pre-programmed timer hit its designated numbers of 06.15. The TV burst into life and the loud, eternally over-enthusiastic breakfast show presenters forced me through my disoriented, groggy transition into sheer bloody wakefulness.

Harsh yellows and oranges from the 24-inch LED screen stung my eyes, acting as my final wake-up call. For the next minute or so I lay there, contemplating what excuse I could use to swerve this meeting and just turn over and re-enter my dreams. The early morning winter darkness indicated that the day was not ready for me yet and my shoulders felt the chill from the outside. Right then, in that moment, the most appealing place to be was under the warm, comfortable covers.

Whatshisname and whosherface off the telly continued to feed me a bad news breakfast of disaster headlines and unnecessary updates of some pointless reality show from their excessively bright studio. My inward annoyance made my eyes leave the screen and seek solace up at the blank white ceiling, and in doing so I proceeded to have what I can only describe as an internal mini-tantrum. On the outside I was still and calm, but on the inside, I was kicking the bedcovers away, arms flailing and screaming my head off. This tantrum happened most mornings when I just couldn't find the motivation to be a fully functioning adult. I lacked the drive to go and earn a living and do the things that I was "supposed to do", according to society's self-proclaimed etiquette. It's not even that my bed was super-comfortable anymore either, the mattress was tired and worn and gave me back pain. But buying a new one was just too much hassle. Plus, I couldn't afford it. My mind was already set to overdrive to think of what else I could do to pay the bills. Hayley, my girlfriend, remained fast asleep next to me.

Maybe if I put more effort into playing the lottery, that could be the way out of this hole I'd found myself in, I thought.

Sometimes, I will tell a story within the story: this is one of those moments. I'm just warning you in case you wonder why I've gone off on a weird tangent.

Hayley and I had met a few years earlier on a free dating app. Our shared trait of being too cheap to invest any money in finding love rather ironically brought us together. I distinctly recall our first date was during Wimbledon, 2013, when we agreed to meet face to face. Andy Murray was on the TV in the bar beating Tommy Robredo in the third round. It was something to watch whilst I waited for Hayley to turn up. The date concluded in the early hours of a warm Friday night outside a south London "dirty chicken burger" shop. I know what you're thinking. "What a romantic guy!" But it was Hayley's idea. "I'm a fried chicken connoisseur, leave this with me," was a line I'll remember forever. You could say she was the original Pengest Munch. She moved in six months later. Since then we've tried to move away from the traditional boyfriend-girlfriend relationship and the social expectations that come with it. There is no breadwinner, we both 'wear the trousers' and it works. My flat transformed from a sad bachelor pad with a huge canvas of Slash from Guns N' Roses in the living room to a more subtle, homely feel. She still has a way-better eye for interiors than I do – I'd never owned a plant before then. With her arrival, they quickly blossomed in our shared living space. Hayley's fast-paced media job in the city sometimes meant we slept alone. She would finish a long night shift and get home and into bed just as I got out of it. We were different. She's a northerner (well, actually a Midlander, but anything north of the M25 was north to me) and I am a somewhat semi-skimmed cockney. A diluted Londoner, you could say. Hayley spoke her mind; I refrained from all conflict. She took risks, I was safety first. She loves rom-coms, I adore gangster films. My eyesight is 20/20, hers was, and still is, abysmal. I turned the volume up; she turned it down. We could play Paula Abdul and the cat from the music video "Opposites Attract", such are our seeming different attitudes to life. Our backgrounds and upbringings were very different too. But, together, we help each other fill in the blanks. Whenever one of us is down, the other is there to pick up the slack. We are a team.

Back in my bedroom, hope appears on the TV in the muscular form of Andi Peters, wearing a tight polo shirt and giving us a gun show at 6.20am. Andi is the positive go-to guy for hyping up a competition on ITV and he was – before the pandemic, that is

– generally filmed in some sunny part of the world giving viewers a glimpse of what life could look like if we were to win his sexy competition. What Andi presented to all of us who were in a morning daze was an opportunity. Andi gave us a chance to make our lives better. He gave us a way out of the drudgery that we had all found ourselves in. His offering that particular morning appealed to me big time. Win £80,000 + A car + A holiday! Within seconds I decided that I'd sell the car, which would maybe raise another £25,000. Before Andi even explained the competition terms and conditions, I'd spent the money. Metaphorically, of course. I'd concluded that this cash (and holiday, don't forget), would make me happier. It would solve all my problems. To be honest, I didn't really know if I had any problems, but the cash would have solved them anyway. The holiday would be a nice break from the job I was bored of as well. Andi gave me the details to text and be in with a chance of winning this prize. I was convinced I had good odds of winning, so I picked up my iPhone – the latest one, of course – which was charging on the floor next to me, opened my messages and typed the word PRIZE. Well, I actually typed ORIZE but the autocorrect helped to explain what I really meant.

My phone vibrated immediately, an automated response confirmed my entry and I was asked whether I'd like to increase my chances of winning by entering again. Of course I'd like to enter again! I texted PRIZE once more, getting the spelling right this time, and within seconds another confirmation came through of my second, and free, third entry.

"Text PRIZE again to submit another entry and get another entry free!" said the message before I'd had a chance to put the phone down and bask in the glory of sorting out any financial woes and the betterment of my immediate future. Why not, I thought? I'd already committed to this competition so swiftly responded with the same message. Five entries now and I'd only paid for three, what a deal! A small sense of achievement washed through me. It became the catalyst that jolted me up and out of bed. I put my phone down on the bedside table satisfied that I'd started the day as all days should – getting stuff for free, kind of. As I stepped into the shower, I didn't even think about the fact that I'd spent just short of a tenner before sunrise.

My weekday morning routine was pretty standard but there was never any room for deviation. To maximise my time in bed, sulking and avoiding the inevitable, I sacrificed time spent actually getting ready for the day ahead. A couple of extra minutes dicking around fixing my hair, ironing a shirt, sorting out my bag or grabbing a bite to eat and that was it, I'd be late to work, a meeting with another company or wherever it was I was going. It was a risky game I played five days a week. If I got it wrong, at the very least there'd be some mild panic and self-deprecation topped with the risk of pulling a hamstring by running to catch a train.

All my clothes were separated out in two rooms. Generally, the things I could fold, such as jeans, shorts and t-shirts that I no longer wore (but couldn't seem to throw away), lived in a dark-brown Ikea HEMNES chest of drawers in the second bedroom down the hall (I had been calling them "Chester drawers" for about thirty years thinking that all drawers were made in Chester until an advert I saw one day totally shattered that belief). Some of the drawers were so filled with clothes that when you pulled one out, another drawer came with it. It was like a crap magic trick. Shirts, suits, trousers, coats and the "fancier" t-shirts lived in the main bedroom inside an absolute monstrosity of a wardrobe. There was just about enough room for a mid-sized human to slide between our king-size bed and the wardrobe to retrieve what was needed. I'd had this wardrobe for about ten years and it wasn't moved an inch because it was so heavy. This brick shit-house of a wardrobe had two sliding doors with oak frames, one with a mirror and one with a black pane of glass inches from the ceiling. It was tall and wide enough to have two decent-length rails on one half and plenty of shelving on the other. The top rail was mine, because Hayley can't reach that high, so she took the bottom one. On the top shelf on the right side of the wardrobe was a stack of shoe boxes, but they didn't contain shoes. Instead, they held old photos, mainly developed from a disposable camera bought once a year and developed at Snappy Snaps. Pictures mainly of drunk people, taken by drunk people. There were faces that I no longer recognised, and the quality of the photography was shocking. The boxes "protecting" these visual memories had also seen better days.

Below that was a 24-inch Sony TV. Its main use was as an alarm clock. This was the one that Andi appeared on that morning. It was the smallest of the three TVs we owned in our south London flat. A cheap aerial booster stood behind it with a constant glowing blue light. Its one job was to improve the picture quality but it generally made no real difference. I left it on because one day I assumed it might work as intended.

The third shelf down held a large box of football kits, gym gear, golf attire and other random accessories. They were all thrown in together like dirty clothes in a laundry basket. I'd not played golf for a few years. Some of it I kept for when my friends and I "played" pub golf. I'd also not played football for quite a while. On the floor of the wardrobe were even more shoe boxes and an assortment of stock from a Converse store. High-tops and low-tops in red, yellow, black, black with orange stars, white with red trim, white with blue trim, white on white, purple tartan felt (yeah, I don't know either) and navy blue were mixed in with others that I designed myself. The Chuck Taylors were stacked up on display so I could make a choice of footwear colour every day. Well, when I say stacked up, I really mean they were just in a pile. In addition to the Converse shoe rainbow I had created were several pairs of smart black and brown shoes, boat shoes, flip-flops and two pairs of slippers, one in regular grey and the other a novelty oversized pair with SpongeBob SquarePants' face on them. I'd never worn slippers, ever.

Standing next to the Chester drawers in the second bedroom was another unit with four shelves. This unit used to reside in the living room, but it had managed to be relegated down the hall somehow. It held all the books, CDs/DVDs and ornaments that didn't fit with the other sources of entertainment, shuffled to the back of the flat away from the main living space. Some of the DVDs had yet to make their way out of the wrapping. A few of them were gifts from various friends back in the day when it was a safe bet as a Christmas or birthday panic buy.

The drum kit accessories from my *PlayStation Guitar Hero* game were resting on top of this unit, wires twisted and pads dusty. One plastic drumstick lay next to them. I couldn't tell you where the other one was. It was lurking somewhere. The books, a collection of dog-eared paperbacks and untouched hardbacks, brought a sense of sophistication and charm to the room; classics such as *1000 Songs You Need to Hear Before You Die* sat on the shelf, waiting for its spine to be cracked. In truth, I had no plans on reading it. I never had the time. There was even a Jamie Oliver *Meals in 15 Minutes* cookbook on the shelf collecting nothing but dust. Jamie, you're in the wrong room, mate.

The unit also contained four binders filled to the brim with "paperwork". The binders, once tidy and rigid, were now a torn and dangerous mess barely able to hold all the expired insurance documents, payslips, pension letters, work contracts, birthday cards and bank statements at bay. A lethal papercut was always just around the corner. Of course, every second or "spare" bedroom needed a sofa bed for that odd occasion when someone stayed over. This sofa bed was situated exactly opposite the drawers, which was where the unplugged third TV hid. It took a few weeks of deliberating before we found the right sofa bed to purchase – the one with the most storage, of course. This uncomfortable and heavy piece of furniture took a few hours to build but it had three really deep drawers to put lots more stuff in, so that was a win. In those drawers squeezed together was some spare bedding, all of Hayley's camera equipment from her university studies, old course paperwork, video recorders and camping gear. That camping gear had seen better days and retained a whiff of a particularly hedonistic Leeds music festival. Over the course of a couple of years, I had to assemble and disassemble that horrible fucking sofa bed half-a-dozen or so times, each time causing rising levels of frustration. I had lost hours of my life to that bastard thing. I'm not bitter about it, honest.

This cosy second bedroom also doubled up as a storage room. Though, in effect, the whole flat was probably a storage room. Hayley's piano-keyboard was still in the box so that was leant up against the unit. In all the years we had been together, I'd never had the joy of hearing her play it. I think I looked in the box once just to confirm there was indeed a keyboard in there. My acoustic guitar sat nicely in the corner leaning up against the sofa bed waiting for someone to strum a tune, no doubt out of tune. It was tucked away in a black padded guitar bag with one front pocket used to store leads, spare strings and other paraphernalia. That pocket was bursting at the seams and one of the music books desperate to escape out the top of it was *Play Guitar with…The Smiths*, an impulse purchase from a music shop after spending an afternoon learning the words to 'Heaven Knows I'm Miserable Now'. That book was used once before I deemed the chords too difficult to learn and it was never looked at again. I haven't played a note for years and it should come as no surprise when I tell you that I also had two other guitars, one a blue hybrid acoustic electric and the other an awesome grey Fender Strat. They both now resided in my parents' loft, collecting dust. They deserved better.

After my shower, I paced between the two bedrooms to get ready. I zoomed back and forth with a different combination of clothes on, dipping into the bathroom to look in the mirror before deciding against what I had chosen. I then went to try and find an ensemble I was happy with that was just the right balance of professional but with an edge, whatever that was, work casual cool, maybe? I'd probably done enough steps walking between the two rooms to win a Fitbit challenge. Eventually I found a blend that suited me and I discarded the losing pieces of attire on the floor. Someone would pick them up eventually.

Running late, I picked up my backpack, which always seemed to be heavy, and threw it over my shoulders. I patted down my pockets to make sure I had everything I needed for the day: wallet, phone, coins, keys, train tickets and earphones. Everything was present and correct. I jogged down the hallway to give Hayley a kiss as she started to rise from her slumber before I turned around and rushed out of the door. The train station was a four-minute walk away, three if I really turned on the afterburners. There was one busy road in the way which I navigated like a pro, weaving between oncoming cars and cyclists who were also in the same rush as me. I started my ascent uphill quicker than usual but without showing too much desperation. I tried not to get into a full-blown run because I would be completely embarrassed in front of a bunch of strangers if I made all that effort only to miss the train. What would these people think of me? I'd be judged and mocked with other commuters sending me subliminal messages saying, "You should have gotten here earlier, mate!"

I began to notice a few people in front of me getting a little bit more of a jog on. It was now clear they were catching the same train and had also decided to cut it close as well. I begrudgingly joined them in a little run, knowing that there was safety in numbers, and we all arrived on the platform as the train doors opened. Perfectly timed, well done, team. I stepped onto the train and gave myself a little bit of a telling-off for spending so long getting ready. I still didn't feel like I'd made the right apparel choices but it was too late to turn back. As I swayed down the carriage to find a seat, I got that feeling of dread that I'd forgotten something important. Every time this happened, I was always transported back to watching a particular Lee Evans stand-up routine. He joked that your brain waited for you to get a far enough distance away from your home before revealing that you had forgotten something. I tried to pre-empt this by patting my pockets again, everything was where it should be. I then opened my bag to see what I could do to appease this feeling but there was too much stuff in there to just look at, so I mentally started to go down the list and bury my hand in to confirm by touch that I had everything I needed. Laptop, yes, water bottle, yes (it's empty but that's fine), notepad and pen, yes and yes. I scratched around at the surface and found some loose coins; I chose to leave them there. Near the coins was a letter that I was supposed to post a few days prior. Work phone, yes, scarf, well, I was wearing one, so I had a spare. Mints, yes, phone charger, yes. I pulled out screwed-up bits of paper that looked like some training material from a few weeks ago and included some scribbles of actions I was supposed to have done (oops). Laptop charger, yes, work pass... Ah.

Shit.

My mind is immediately transported back home where I pictured an item on the floor in a pair of trousers that I'd discarded only moments earlier. My laminated work pass and fob. I called myself a fucking idiot because now I'd need a chaperone to get in and out of the office all day or else I'd have to lurk around and tailgate people. Tailgating was frowned upon in my department, as you can imagine.

The forgetting of the pass was not a big deal in itself, I was more concerned with what people would think of me as I started to project some awkward scenarios of me being locked outside or something. Propelling myself into the make-believe future, I tried to figure out a solution. I suppose I could wait for someone to come outside and, when they did, I could pretend to be finishing up a call, grab the door as they leave, and that way look important because the call needed to be taken outside (classic managerial move). I was clearly also far too important and busy being important to show my pass. The perfect plan. The phone had better not ring as I'm holding it to my ear though, I thought to myself.

I rearranged the bag's contents to a somewhat more organised hierarchy and zipped the bag up. At least I knew what I was missing, but that slight inconvenience irked me and I questioned my ability as this progressive leader with all the ideas. What does it say to others if I couldn't get my own shit together? Never mind, I'll be able to buy all the passes I wanted when Andi hands me an oversized cheque for £80,000.

In case you were expecting a twist at the end of the book, no, I didn't win.

Amanda had invited me to the local coffee shop. Her plan was to go through the fine print of what a "career break" looked like. It was a refreshing change from the same old windowless box meeting room we usually gravitated to. Amanda was super-cool. I'd worked with her for many years across a couple of companies doing a similar role. We had a mentor-friend relationship where every meeting was greeted with a respectful hug rather than a transactional handshake. She was all for looking after her people and always encouraged me to go out and experience new career options. I didn't anticipate her raising any concerns about me disappearing for ten months.

Before we departed for the coffee shop, I waited patiently outside the office doors for her to finish another meeting. She was already a few minutes late, but I had no choice but to linger and say hello to some co-workers that I'd not seen in a few weeks. They shot me a smile and went about their day holding their recently purchased sandwich from the nearby supermarket and, because it was lunch time, their priority was their food and I didn't want to cause them any more delay. I know how "hangry" people can get. A few minutes went by and I started to feel the windchill from the nearby coast. I appreciated the sun's rays, so I turned my face towards the direction of the bright beams to absorb the warmth. I'd chosen a thin jumper, grey suit jacket and dark-blue skinny jeans as my fashion of choice for the visit, they were my main shield from the cold alongside a thin grey scarf that I wore as much indoors as outdoors. An even thinner scarf was buried in the bottom of my bag, but I chose to leave it there. Amanda had not seen me for a few months, so I didn't want her first question to be "Are you wearing two scarfs?" In that moment, my backpack felt heavy on my shoulders, so I reached up and gave a quick stretch to ease a small ache near the base of my neck. It wasn't long before I saw Amanda stroll out the double doors with a book and pen in hand, apologising for her delay. She was better prepared for the outside than I was, she had a long thick black coat on which almost reached the floor. She simultaneously pulled out two mobile phones to check any work or home problem she had to solve before we started our walk to the cafe.

Once inside our quaint and cosy destination, Amanda headed straight for the counter and ordered a glass of wine. As it was past midday, I felt it was just about OK to order a beer and we found a table for two by the window. She didn't hesitate to get the bill. This place was a hotbed for lunch-time work meetups so as I took my seat, I was greeted by a wave from the other side of the room from colleagues who I'd not seen for a few months. I waved back and mouthed, "I'll come and see you in a bit," followed by a thumbs up which gave the indication that I was busy and to leave us be. I took my bag off my shoulders, giving the right one a quick and deep rub, as I placed it carefully underneath the table. Amanda whipped off her coat and settled into her chair. Before I had even sat down, she raised her large glass of red offering a cheers and I swiftly accepted. I picked up my pint, clinked her large glass and swallowed a mouthful of cold lager, my first meal of the day. I had sacrificed a peaceful morning breakfast, remember. I enjoyed the sensation of the beer and pulled up a pew.

Before we got into the details of the sabbatical, we took the opportunity to share the current challenges the two of us both faced. We both agreed we were super-busy and had loads going on. We skirted through the unwritten rule of measuring up our ever-growing list of things to do in order to portray our individual importance and subconsciously agreed we must be busy at all times otherwise we've not contributed enough. Everything was a priority and each situation was as important as the next. There was a sense of, "It would get better when…", but inside we both knew there would always be that next challenge, task or project around the corner and, deep down, we were probably guilty of accepting that rather than doing anything about it. I glanced down to see the scribbled notes in her pad; her handwriting had never been the neatest but the notes and haphazard presentation indicated a lack of control. I recognised that because my own workbook looked similar. The first few pages were neat and tidy and then random words, scribbled-out passwords, phone numbers and names of people were littered everywhere. Attempted 'To Do' lists were started but then abandoned. Is that what success looked like? We talked through the logistics of the sabbatical and she listed all the terms and conditions that she was required to give me before the news got communicated out to everyone else in the department. I knew I'd not receive any benefits or compensation throughout the break, no salary and no other contributions. Amanda made sure I was fully aware of what to expect during that period. Pretty much nothing. There was a half promise though – my position would be held open for a period but if the shit was to hit the fan while I was away, they'd have to fill my role and I'd have to look for something else upon my return. My responsibilities were not so important that they couldn't have lived without me for a few months, hidden away in the layers of middle management. We didn't say it but we both knew the chances of me returning were slim. For the first time, Amanda could see that something had started to change within me, and deep down I knew I was feeling unfulfilled. Once we were done with the formalities, we got to talking about the reason for the adventure itself.

"It's great, by the way, and I'm all for it," she said, half convincingly. "But what's making you feel the need to take some time out?"

I let Amanda know that I'd never taken a proper break in

all my adult working life, more than fifteen years. The odd one-week holiday here and there but never a substantial time-out from grinding, or just life in general. Everything was always just flashing by. Time was going by so quickly that I had never stopped to see where I was going. And it was Hayley's idea really, she was able to recognise that she needed a break and called it out to me that I could do with one as well.

"I've started to feel as if there is more I should be doing, more I could be accomplishing, but I'm not sure what," I told Amanda, in an attempt to be profound. "I want to find out before it's too late."

The last couple of years had been testing. Hayley had been through some tough times and she just needed to jump off the hamster wheel. After having a panic attack on the Tube during rush hour, she became regularly fatigued. Her job in the media demanded long shifts, day and night. Not only did it require 'being on' mentally for the best part of the day or night but it was physically draining as well. This continuous fatigue then led to an appointment at the doctors, followed by another and then another. The fatigue of the job, mixed with the stress it caused as well as the panic attack, led doctors to believe she had some form of epilepsy and to counter the risk of seizures (she hadn't had any, ever), she would need to regularly take suppressive medication. Not only did she have to go through this new and surprising diagnosis, she then had to give back her driving licence and refrain from getting behind the wheel for at least a year. It was a significant blow for a strong, independent woman to have part of her independence taken away from her.

Was this what a career was supposed to be like until retirement?

We understood the risks and went along with what the

experts recommended. In an attempt to remedy this and dial down the feeling of chaos, stress and uncertainty, Hayley quit her job and the accompanying painful commute. In a bid to calm it all down further, we temporarily moved to the coast for a year to try and gather a sense of calm. Brighton had always been a sentimental place for us, it was where we had one of our first dates. In an attempt to be romantic and spontaneous, I took her on the fifty-foot Ferris wheel for some views over the coast and surrounding areas. This was before I had spilled the beans of my fear of heights. It was a pleasurable experience for her (and super-uncomfortable one for me), so we had fond memories of it. That, mixed with the cosmopolitan feel of the vibrant community and an opportunity to absorb the sound of the ocean waves on a daily basis, seemed like our kind of area and the ideal place to move our focus into setting up a new and exciting chapter of our lives.

Hayley's health was the start of the shift, the start of feeling unfulfilled, and the start of beginning a new way of life. We had moved all our stuff down to the coast on Halloween 2015 with giddy optimism and squeezed it into our new, but smaller, rented two-bedroom home. We decided to let our friends rent our actual home in south London for a short time so we could test this new idea without losing our property. The second bedroom (or "spare room") once again became a holding pen for all the junk we had no immediate use for. Grand ideas of that space being a little music room or somewhere more creative were quickly dashed and swamped by the unopened boxes and wall art we hadn't yet got around to finding a place for. The BESTÅ Ikea TV unit that no longer fitted in our new living room was broken down and leant up against the wall. Because that TV unit didn't fit where it was supposed to, we had to, of course, buy a new one. Random bits of wood that accompanied us on the move were slid under the bed or hidden behind clothes and other cabinets to avoid having to make a decision about them.

Once we settled in Brighton, Hayley found herself a new

job, which meant a brand-new career in a new industry. New people to get to know, a new (quicker) commute, new systems and processes to learn, a new culture, everything new. I had no intention of changing jobs at that time, that would have been far too scary. I was also waiting for some indication of internal career opportunities that could maybe materialise, so wanted to stick around and potentially not miss out on any of those.

That was me once again waiting for stuff to happen rather than pro-actively participating in my own life.

Because I stayed in the same job in the same office, my commute time and cost of travel from Brighton to Croydon had trebled and I was reliant on one of the most unreliable train services in the UK, Southern Rail (or as most commuters liked to call them, Southern Fail). Some days I would get stuck on the way home near Gatwick airport, some evenings I'd have to wait for a replacement bus service to arrive. The constant strikes by the train drivers were called "the worst transport disruption in the last twenty years", by many media outlets. From memory, this was all caused because there was a dispute about who closed the train doors. I'm sure there was more to it than that but honestly, I didn't really care, I was missing out on valuable time with my partner in our new environment getting to know our new surroundings. I hated the stress that excessive public transport commuting injected into my already busy life. For some, including me, it was the only bit of calm before entering the rat race. Reporters from the BBC and ITV also joined a number of journeys and I would regularly be squashed against a door and someone else's sweaty armpit on a carriage as they shuffled around with a camera and microphone looking for crazy reactions from commuters that they could broadcast. Commuters were raging and properly losing their shit on a daily basis, I tried to stay composed, but it was hard not to get caught up in all the fury. I ignored all opportunities to comment on national TV, however.

Whilst I was huffing and puffing and wasting energy on fighting with Southern Rail, Hayley's less chaotic new job, coordinating classes at the local university, turned into a bit of a nightmare. Being talked down to by academics daily wasn't really floating her boat and after a number of months taking shit for something she had no interest in, her resignation came as no surprise. She didn't want to work for horrible people, and completing mundane tasks in exchange for less money than she deserved. All the while, her previous work would regularly check in and remind her how much of an asset she was to them, clearly working hard to try and talk her into a return. Hayley probably clocked then that there was more to life than tolerating an unfulfilling job to pay off debts we had collected from buying more stuff we didn't need. That also coincided with further monitoring trips to the doctors after various types of tablets hadn't really done anything. Hayley was feeling better when she wasn't necking the prescribed pills and it was quickly confirmed that she had been misdiagnosed and actually had no signs of epilepsy. That misdiagnosis was massively frustrating due to the changes she and I had made to our lives and it was just another thing that we felt helpless about that negatively influenced our lives.

But, ultimately, the seed of a new way of living – *being* – had been planted in our minds.

In the end, we left Brighton after only a year, more confused than when we arrived. We ended up moving back into our old flat, this time with an extra year's worth of stuff accumulated and an increased anger about the lack of control we had. Maybe that experiment had gone a bit pear-shaped and we were destined to live a life reacting to shit happening to us and tackling the challenges born out of our own crap decision making. Or maybe, it was exactly what we needed? This jolt of trying to physically shift our lives somewhere else to cause a positive reaction clearly didn't work as planned, but the intention was there. In trying to move away from the madness, clutter and the feeling of a lack of control in London, all we ended up doing was just bringing it all down to Brighton with us. Something quite significant needed to change in order for us to gain more fulfilment and control in life. So, we agreed that taking some time out from both our careers to travel and step away from just drifting along and reacting retroactively to life events would be exactly what we wanted. What we needed.

Back in the coffee shop, as expected, Amanda was cool about all the reasons I wanted to leave and said that travelling was a wonderful thing to do after the year we had endured. We clinked glasses again to celebrate the future but this time they were both nearly empty. She let me know that she'd send an email out to everyone letting them know that I would be taking an extended break. She checked the time on her watch and polished off the last glug of wine. This prompted me to knock down the last few drops of my brunch beer and as she got up to put her coat on, I took the empty glasses back to the counter. I waved to the rear of the room where my other colleagues were still nattering, and they gave me a wave back. Our stroll back to the office was at a quicker pace than the one that brought us to the coffee shop as Amanda's mind had shifted to the next thing, the next person she had to speak to, the next virtual fire she had to put out.

Outside the office, I hugged Amanda. As she disappeared back through the revolving doors, I stood outside, contemplating what had just occurred. I dropped Hayley a text to confirm all was good and that the sabbatical was approved. We had passed the point of no-return. Then, as I needed to piss desperately, and I was regretting not asking Amanda to let me in the building one final time, I immediately started to digest the magnitude of what I had just requested. I immediately went through a whole bunch of mixed emotions consisting mainly of excitement and fear. I was suddenly excited for the adventure on the horizon but supremely fearful and uncomfortable of the new unknown. Part of me wanted to just carry on with life as normal, tell Amanda it was all a big mistake and forget the whole damn thing. I had invested so much time and energy into my current set-up that walking off and letting go felt wrong, even if I convinced myself it would only be temporary. If I kept waiting, I would eventually get what I wanted, I thought, but I wasn't sure if I even knew what

I wanted anyway. My negative thinking was disrupted by a group of post-lunching colleagues saying hello as they approached the building. I tailgated behind one of them and took the lift back up to the floor where my desk for the day was. My laptop lid was up and ready for work. I, on the other hand, was not.

Only eight more months to go…

2. Planning Is Half the Fun

The build-up of anticipation, the endless possibilities, the excitement of adventure and misadventure was on the horizon. There was only one thing for it, a perfectly curated spreadsheet. The irony was not lost on me as I opened my work laptop to help with putting together a plan of escape from said work. How naughty. I did have my own laptop, but it was a dinosaur compared to the top-of-the-range, super-speedy HP one the company had provided me. It was also an inconvenience to retrieve the relic, buried in the footstool underneath two of Hayley's laptops that she hadn't used for years. One of which I'm sure was broken. Going hunting in the footstool would have been too much of a chore, I would have had to shift a special edition Simpsons Monopoly that I bought from a toy shop at Disneyland in 2001 and a deluxe Scrabble with spinning board. No letters had been laid on the triple word score for about six years. Half the Monopoly pieces were missing but I kept the game anyway. Who knows, they may turn up someday (aren't we all searching for the missing pieces?). There was also a likelihood that I'd have got drawn into reading old birthday cards while I was there, reminiscing on the past and reading old messages. Lifting those items up would have caused the poker chips to fly everywhere and all the tangled spare ethernet cables, HDMI leads and redundant chargers would further embroil themselves with anything else lifted up and out. The footstool barely closed as it was, that slight bit of space between the top and the storage compartment was a tease, but we'd lived with it springing slightly ajar when there was no pressure on it. Eventually, whatever was keeping it from shutting properly would get worn down, so it rested perfectly. Organising the junk in there was never a priority and it would remain there for a good while yet.

As I sank into my deep sofa, I began to lose myself to the glow of a bunch of blank spreadsheet cells. With planning on the front of my mind, and work stuck at the back, I made the decision of naming a number of tabs so I could break down each part of our adventure. It might have still been eight months off then, but it felt the right thing to do after starting to mentally clock off and effectively handing in my (temporary) resignation. The Google worksheet menu was different to the Microsoft Excel options I was used to at work but it didn't take me long to get comfortable with my new palatte. 'Travel Master' was labelled on the first worksheet, closely followed by headers on the columns unveiling something of a timeline. I started to imagine driving at just below the speed limit through stunning landscapes. The warmth of the outside was countered with the air conditioning of the hire car and whilst appreciating the surroundings, I'd be nodding along to a local radio station's playlist.

'Date', 'Country', 'Town', 'Days' and 'Transport' got typed out in Verdana and, as the headers, were highlighted in bold. 'Average Temperature', 'Exchange Rate', 'Visa' and 'Injections' joined the row as I cleaned up the spelling and arranged the text so it was all formatted appropriately. Something stopped me from adding 'Cost' until the very end, just out of sight on the sliding scale, far enough away so I didn't have it ruin my spreadsheet party. I procrastinated for about ten minutes in an attempt to think of something witty to call this file creation. 'Travels' sounded a bit shit, but it was the most creative thing I could come up with in the moment. In fact, I never did change the title:'Travels' remained attached to that document and is still on my laptop today, as a reminder of the planning, and it actually became massively useful when writing this book.

"Right, where shall we go first?" I asked Hayley as she concentrated deeply on her *Harry Potter* book, decompressing from the day.

"I don't mind, but I'd love to go to Myanmar at some point," she responded excitably. Following some further daydreaming, discussion and a bit more research, I started to populate the spreadsheet with European capitals, Far Eastern countries I'd never been to and parts of North America I'd only ever seen in the movies. We'd been invited to a couple of weddings over the planned time away – one in Slovenia and another in Jamaica – and if we were smart, we could use those special events to pivot and springboard around the world. With the right timeline and some jiggery-pokery on the cash front, attendance at those special events would enhance our soul-finding adventure. Ljubljana, Yangon, Montego Bay, Las Vegas, Toronto and Copenhagen all got added as starters for intended destinations that had been discussed over the previous few weeks. I suggested to Hayley the possibility of a stay with some distant Canadian relatives in Halifax, Nova Scotia, and then clicked away to send them a message on Facebook to see if they were up for it. I'd not spoken to them or seen them since I was about nine so there would be lots of catching up to do. I was unconsciously sitting up and my neck leant towards the laptop almost trying to propel myself into the future as my face was being pulled into the glow of the screen. Reaching a new level of excitement, the burdens of the day, the week, started to evaporate. I could almost taste the freedom of orchestrating days in faraway lands as my fingers hurriedly transcribed details of festivals, treks, high-priority stop-offs and opportunities to volunteer along with rough estimates on how long, and how much, to spend in each new place. Sacrificing detail and accuracy, I tabbed between a dozen screens that had now appeared through various Google searches and swift rabbit holes, my attention now so thinly spread I'd sent my brain into a heightened state of distress. Far removed from my initial structure and planning, I peeled my eyes away from the screen for a few seconds to give them some respite and that's all it took to fully distract me. A quick scan around the living room and my eyes wanted to dart here, there and everywhere looking at all the colours of the many books and DVDs as well as the shimmer of the shiny trinkets on top of the TV cabinet. I ran my fingers through my hair whilst simultaneously letting out a big sigh as I caught a reflection of myself in the window.

I'd lost focus. My attention was now on the batch of vinyl I'd recently bought, conscious that I hadn't really made use of the record player for a while. The speakers on it were pretty poor so I used my old PC speakers and subwoofer instead; different colour wires were all intertwined and dangling under the table. Hayley hated visible wiring. On the one hand, the homemade music station gave off a hipster vibe with the vintage records, but the mid-90s chunky AIWA speakers completely clashed and overwhelmed the record player. I'd somehow acquired two pairs of those speakers, the others being underneath my legs in the footstool. As my eyes continued to pace the room, I felt a real sense of guilt because I was a massive music fan and real music fans listened to music on vinyl, right? Or maybe that was just my perception. I'd neglected them and new purchases of albums I already owned on other formats sat un-played and unloved. *The Miseducation of Lauryn Hill* was most visible alongside Marvin Gaye's *What's Going On* and Sade's *Diamond Life*. A dusty old two-pence piece rested on the needle to keep it weighed down to reduce the risk of any skipping, an old trick my dad taught me.

The speakers bothered me. I shouldn't be relying on twenty-year-old computer speakers to fulfil my musical needs, I thought to myself. Probably buying some "proper" ones would rest easier with me so I could fully enjoy the experience of listening to my records. If I just bought more accessories, I thought, I'd be happy and only then could I really enjoy the distinct sound of the dust particles and scratches that gave each vinyl its romantic crackle. I imagined that one day, when I hosted my dream house party, friends would be so impressed with the vinyl offering that they would flick through the collection and put some of their favourite tunes on my record player. They'd be able to experience something that maybe they'd not experienced for some time, holding each one carefully and looking closely for the grooves when placing the needle. I'd have to wander around behind them putting the records back in their sleeves as in their excitement they would, of course, forget to put some back in their rightful place. They would ask me questions about my collection, and I would get excited to answer. We'd all have a sweet time and I'd be able to offer this retro vinyl record-playing experience to them. Of course, I hadn't hosted a house party for years. Certainly not one where music was played loud or at all, but I didn't worry about that. I picked my phone up and Googled "speakers that go well with record players". I didn't know exactly what I was looking for, but I felt the need to buy something. The jargon and technical specs of the speakers confused me so I headed towards a top-ten list on some blog so someone else could tell me what I was supposed to like. I spent forty-five minutes reading about the pros and cons of clarity, bass frequencies and transparency and got lost in a world of high-end gear that was out of my price range. Put off by some of the numbers and lingo, I decided to leave that search for another day and instead went to find the latest thing people were getting livid about on Twitter. This doomscrolling was no good for my mental health but I did it anyway.

I was once again distracted as my laptop screen changed from a clear table with minimal scrambled content to the company's logo against a blue screen. The touchpad had clearly been untouched for a decent amount of time as I'd drifted off down a Twitter timeline rabbit hole and lost all that initial travel planning excitement. My state of flow had abandoned me and would not return for a while. Distraction and loss of focus had started to become my lifestyle. Travel planning seemed like a chore again and without making any effort to log off properly I closed the laptop lid with a tad more force than normal and turned on the TV.

3. Busy, Always Busy

Before Hayley and I went travelling, I liked having lots of things to do. Well, at least, I thought I did. It gave me what I thought was a sense of achievement and importance. The busier I was, the more important I felt (and appeared). That's all I knew, that's all I saw. The higher up the imaginary career ladder people got, the busier they seemed. That is what I had been unintentionally programmed to understand as successful. Late nights, working weekends and an unmanageable volume of emails equalled winning, right? Hustle, hustle, hustle, hard work. Spare time was for slackers.

Work was always busy enough. It was not physically demanding but it was often mentally draining. The team and I were constantly doing lots of "work"; but I wasn't convinced it all added that much value to others, but we did it anyway. No one really questioned it. We just filled our days with meetings and emails talking about the same things over and over again. No one ever reached the end of their To-Do list; it just got longer with more things to get done. I still wonder if anyone actually knows what happens at the end of their To-Do list? Is there a prize? Do you get a parade? I want a parade.

In modern corporate office life, everything takes an age to sign off. By the time it gets signed off it's usually too late to be of use. A colleague once said to me, "Getting things to change was like turning a tanker ship." And they were right. It took a good deal of effort to just stay on top of things – treading water – that then became the only priority.

The regular travelling back and forth to the office HQ in Bournemouth was starting to become tiring as well. On their own, the journeys were not too bad, but stack them up, and I suddenly had less time and motivation to do the actual job. Back then, I never really figured out how to say no to things and kept piling tasks on top of tasks. I'd got accustomed to always playing catch-up and wrestling with a million and one things to do. I was programmed to believe that was the way it was supposed to be, and because I saw everyone else do it, I felt out of place for not being overwhelmed. Even though I was getting buried under piles of 'yes', I still went searching for fulfilment by doing more.

In an effort to increase the hustle and fill those empty blocks of time outside of the nine-to-five, a few years ago, I volunteered to host a music show on a new local radio station. Because learning to play the guitar wasn't hard enough, I thought I'd throw something else into the mix and expand my passion for music and discovering new unsigned talent by sharing some tunes to a small online audience.

My love for music comes from my mum and dad, Rose and Ian, and hearing them play their favourite songs as they drove my brother Gary, and I to school. They were musicians too, and most evenings as they rehearsed for their next gig with their band, Rainbow's End, I would hear my mum sing and listen as my dad smashed the shit out of the drums. I bet the neighbours loved us.

As a budding DJ, I enjoyed the whole process of researching what songs I would play, speaking into the microphone and working all the equipment in the studio. When the mics went down and the show finished, I was spent. The blast of energy was so draining I would often be quiet and tired for hours after. Putting on the extroverted persona was great, but as a natural introvert, I needed to step away from people and the hyped-up state of it all to recharge. As the months went on, the show became more popular – more and more people started to tune in, much to my amazement – and I invited my friends and other guests to join me on-air and share their different musical tastes. The whole thing was just fun with no real end goal in sight. I started to grow more confident being the emcee-DJ-presenter and it then went from my friends being on the show to actual musicians being on it who played live in the studio. Within two years it went from just me and friends for two-hours playing what we wanted every other Saturday morning, to a Thursday night slot every week, structured sections and a guest artist either being interviewed or playing live. I was regularly sent music to play from PR executives, industry types and artists, plus I would go out and proactively look for songs that would fit the style of the show.

My friend Jenna, who was also a new-music buff, somehow discovered that a small music venue in east London was looking for a gig/curator booker. I didn't really know what that was, but we went along and scoped it out. The music space was a good size, about a hundred people could comfortably enjoy seeing some live acts there. It was in one of the trendiest parts of town and we would be given a small budget to spend for each show. Although we had never done anything like this before, we agreed to give it a go and just figured it all out as we went along. We shared the responsibilities of it all and with our newly found knowledge of the local music scene and connection with the radio station, we set up a music project called Souterrain, from the French word for underground.

Souterrain remained somewhat popular and the venues we were hosting shows at wanted us to double the volume of live gigs we hosted, and it was still just Jenna and me. The radio show was still going strong and I spent a few hours each week editing it down and making it into a podcast. We curated two live gigs a month at the same venue, one mid-week and one primetime, Saturday night. I had spent just under a grand on my own DJ equipment and learnt how to mix and scratch. We were booking shows at other venues, curating small festivals, writing for music blogs and providing a coaching and development service to unsigned artists from all over the world. Our social media needed daily monitoring and we were regularly designing posters, flyers and teaser videos to upcoming shows. We'd take most of the photos and video for advertising, which also needed posting and editing. My walks from the flat to the office in Croydon were dominated by listening to songs from London artists and surrounding areas who fit into the emerging and unsigned category. Artists that we could "get". Our search for local music grew so intense that the SoundCloud and Spotify algorithms no longer suggested any mainstream music. We were sent so much music and I felt obliged to listen to it all. A lot of it was, let's say, shit. My lunch times were regularly taken up by responding to emails from artists, managers, agents, venues and sound engineers, negotiating payments, set lengths, times, dates, available equipment, all sorts. I'd started to create stock templates so I could just copy all the information over. If there was a break in my schedule during my "day job", I created as many online events as time would allow. Jenna often stayed late at her work to produce the visuals that accompanied each gig and were the face of this brand we had created. We both had full-time jobs, were both in relationships, both had lives that required attendance. Souterrain had become a second full-time job that rewarded us with a bit of chump change. Champagne dreams, lemonade money.

Even though it was a slog at times, I still found great fulfilment in curating these gigs and turning a passion into something where I could, in my own small way, influence and take part in the music industry. I didn't have the talent to be in a band, so it was the next best thing. I attended as many gigs as I could and hung out with some amazing artists, some of whom I'm now proud to call my friends, but I sensed that Souterrain had a shelf life. However, because it was my passion project, and I'd invested time into it, I dismissed the possibility of it all ending because I didn't think I'd like the outcome of letting it go. Subsequently, I ignored all the warning signs and just carried on carrying on.

There were always things that needed doing, whether that was at work, with all the strands of Souterrain, DIY at home and keeping the house clean and tidy on a surface level, having a social life, seeing friends and family, going to gigs, doing all the travel research, shopping for stuff I didn't need, managing my debts, trying to find time to exercise, it was non-stop. I was aware that I was choosing to do all of those things, but I didn't think I was aware of the impact it was having. When someone asked me how I was doing, my default reaction was always to choose one of the following – "stacked" or "slammed".

Maybe I was just addicted to being busy?

4. Start At The Middle

A week or so after my meeting with Amanda, I watched the condensation in the corners of the bedroom window start to drip onto the freshly cleaned windowsill. Sneaking my left foot out from under the covers I felt the freshness of this new late winter Sunday morning, but that small taste of cold was needed to calibrate my body temperature, warm and cosy underneath the heavy duvet. Rolling my left ankle anti-clockwise at the same time caused a jarring but painless double crack. That poor ankle had taken a battering down the years, reckless football tackles from eager opposition players (and sometimes teammates) as well as self-inflicted injuries had seen it turn a multitude of colours as the human body had done its thing, repairing itself time and time again, leaving extra bits of scar tissue on each occasion. There was no longer pain, but I could feel imperfections.

Down by the side of the bed was my iPad and, like a twitch, it's the first thing I involuntarily reached for, giving my body a small stretch at the same time. Following some exciting conversations with Hayley about what activities we could do whilst away, I was motivated and eager to get something substantial booked for our journey. This was an opportunity for us both to just step away from the day-to-day hustle, explore the world a bit more and expand our experience of life, so I made it my mission to not get out of bed until I'd actually done something about it. Yes, I was aware of the irony.

Hayley and I had been invited to our friend's wedding at the beautiful Lake Bled, Slovenia, in August 2017, so we decided to use their special day as the jumping-off point into the rest of our trip. We roughly plotted out a plan to spend August to November in Asia and then December to April(ish) 2018 across Canada and the US, plus a couple of months on the back end to work out later. It was a back-of-a-cigarette-packet type plan, but a plan, nonetheless. The lure of Southeast Asia made us want to prioritise Myanmar, Thailand, Laos, Vietnam, Cambodia and

Singapore first, and we powered on to make it happen without too much thought.

Whilst Hayley had focused her efforts on national parks and researching volunteering opportunities, I took control of cities and logistics. Finding the cheapest price or a cheeky discount became a bit of an obsession. With a glass of water in one hand, I visited the same flight comparison sites I'd been looking at for the previous two weeks to see if there had been any change in price. There hadn't. I cleared my cookies one last time to stop the bots thinking that flights to Yangon were getting popular and subsequently put the price up. Hours of research on prices later and £733 for two was the cheapest I could find, so I shouted out to Hayley, who was now up and working in the background, that I felt I was ready to book our first big flight. She yelled the all-clear and within a matter of seconds the remaining part of my wages for the month got obliterated as I hit confirm. A minute or so later, an email confirmation arrived and suddenly our trip into the known unknown all felt very real. The text was bold and clear: 7am flight with Adria Airways from Ljubljana arriving in Frankfurt at 08.25. Transfer to China Airlines 11.20pm long haul arriving in Taipei, Taiwan, at 06.10am the following day. The final transfer was 07.05am that got us to our destination of Yangon, the largest city in Myanmar, bang on 9am. I moved the email into a special folder in a new account that Hayley had set up just for this trip. The email address was extra-long, as was the most ridiculously difficult password to remember.

"Hay!' I shout.

"What?"

What's the password again for the travel email?"

"Travel, four, as in number four, reals yo, reals is with a z instead of an s, all one word, exclamation mark, question mark, 2017... 18."

"For fuck's sake," I mumbled under my morning breath.

"What?"

"Nothing."

Before I had even brushed my teeth that morning I felt that a poignant moment, that first step towards something significant, had been achieved. All the pre-game talk had ended and the first piece on the chess board had been moved. It was exciting and a little scary all at the same time. I could see the start of the adventure. Of course, it was not official until the spreadsheet was updated. I tapped into the document and filled in the blank cells with a sense of pride. No spelling mistakes, no auto-corrects, it was all done and official. My attention swiftly turned to locking in some activities to do. One thing I had been researching was a three-day trek from Kalaw to Inle Lake, covering about 60km of the Myanmar countryside. The evenings were spent staying in local villages and the whole thing just looked like an unforgettable experience. I pictured us both sitting on the floor around a fire in the middle of nowhere eating home-cooked cuisine as we tried to speak to the people in the village. I imagined our guide translating as they handed us both a small glass of some unknown local drink. I ended up smelling it and pulling a face as I'm blown away by the almost petrol-like pungent aroma which, of course, everyone laughs at. They waited to anticipate my reaction as I took a sip and the contents are so strong that I coughed and spluttered whilst my eyes widened, swiftly followed by huge belly laughs from the locals. Their homemade liquor makes the tourists pull faces and that provided them entertainment that they never got bored with. No one knew what each other was saying but because of the flow of alcohol, we ended up laughing and hugging anyway, pointing and making shapes to best describe what we are trying to convey. We all clinked glasses and, for those few hours, we were all together, as a community. Same-same but different. I pictured the guide leaning over to me and saying something like, "Too much of this will fuck you up". The drink was awful, but we all gulped it on down anyway. We lost track of time and our guide informed us that we were leaving at 6am. He or she broke down the etiquette for using the washing facilities, a pan of cold water and a hole in the floor, as well as what time the locals would wake starting their day farming for essentials. I pictured us grabbing a few pictures of us all together and heading to bed. In the distance was the faint chatter of family life; they had very little apart from a cow that helped with carrying buckets up and down the hill, a few clothes washed each day and each other. They are content, it was a simple life and they had enough. The moonshine probably helped put them in a good mood too!

The thundering rattle of the 09.08am train to London Victoria outside the bedroom window knocked me out of this daydream and I finished adding the final flight details to the spreadsheet. Once it was done, I set myself a deadline. Five more minutes in bed and then I was getting up. It had been a productive morning already, I deserved a long, hot shower to celebrate. As I researched further into the details of the trek, a selection of online reviews recommended certain times of the year to go. I suddenly noticed there was a consistent theme that the best time to go was not the same time as we were planning to be there.

Interesting, I pondered out loud. I wonder why that was?

My face suddenly started to flush with red blood cells. You know the feeling. My touch on the screen got heavier, as I raced onto another website hunting for reassurance from other reviews. A slight wave of pressure started in my shoulders and slowly moved its way down to my chest. My breathing had become inconsistent, fluttered, out of sync. My razor-sharp focus was blurred slightly but I fixated on the dates these reviews were written alongside any other references of time. The majority were written in January, February or March.

OK.

I uncovered one reviewer on the final page of comments that mentioned going in August and referencing something about the rain. One day, apparently it was so torrential they had to turn back. They used the word "deluge". Another reviewer mentioned the rain and it filled me full of self-doubt and anxiety. Somewhere in the back of my mind, hidden away behind a stack of other anxieties, was half a memory of a conversation with someone about the wet season. Also, there was that one negative comment I'd spotted that becomes amplified over all the other positive ones. These two random things combined spelt trouble. I Googled "Myanmar rainy season". I wasn't feeling lucky.

Rainy – June to October is monsoon season with high rainfall.
Oh, fuck off, Google.

In denial, I amended my search to try and get the answer I wanted but it all led back to the same information. Bottom-line was that it was highly likely to be pissing it down the majority of the time we were in southeast Asia.

I'd fucked it. The first big booking and I'd cocked it up.

I frantically checked the email received about the flights and read through the FAQ document that accompanied it. Deep down I knew I could be in trouble – picking the cheaper option rarely left room for second chances. Of course, no refund for flight cancellations. Any of it. Fantastic. They may as well have called it the "fuck you" document.

At this point, I realised I probably should have paused at all the bits on the website that read 'Are you sure?' or 'Important information, please read'. My impatience to get something booked had massively backfired. I shouted out to Hayley and revealed the balls-up.

I was now over my five-minute deadline and I was still in bed talking it out with Hayley as to what we could possibly do to remedy this situation. She had her hands on her head. I was so embarrassed that I lost all rational sense and blamed everything else apart from my poor research. It was the website's fault, it was the airline's fault, it was the iPad's fault. I quickly turned into the victim of the piece. I created a weather column on the spreadsheet, but it remained blank. I sat up in bed, because that's how serious it was, and tried to call the airline, but the hold times were ridiculous, and I hung up within ten minutes. While on hold I considered calling my bank and making up some story to get them to pity on me so they could call back the payment somehow. All sorts of madness went through my mind, from swerving the payment and pleading ignorance to just swallowing the loss, to faking identity fraud. Though I'm not sure Amanda would have approved of that one.

For some reason, we had decided to spend three to four months in rain and then fly over to Canada and the US to spend another three to four months in the winter, returning to the UK at the back end of our own winter. Brilliant! I was sure it would still be great, but it was not really the vision we had in mind. What was I thinking?! Well, the truth of the matter is I wasn't, not clearly anyway. Impatience had got the better of me.

For me, booking the trip had become another thing cluttering up my mind. A job on the To-Do list to be ticked off. A chore.

Problem unsolved, I jumped out of bed and discarded the duvet like a piece of trash. I was so angry at myself for making a costly mistake that had been so easily avoidable. But I was a problem solver, I thought to myself, so I believed I could work out a solution without losing a stack of cash.

The water in the shower was instantly cold so I quickly withdrew my arm away from the dial and waited for it to heat up, letting out a huff of annoyance at the same time. Once warm enough, I stepped inside the shower cubicle and let the hot water splash over my head as I looked down to the floor, hoping it would wash away my frustration and disappointment. I never used to be like this, I thought to myself. I used to be always on the ball, paid attention to the devil in the details, I was methodical, measured. It was my strength, well, it was supposed to be. I never made these types of mistakes. Until recently. Where had my patience and the ability to provide calm to a situation gone? What had happened? It was not just one mistake that I could put down to being tired or for lack of research. It was a small holding pattern of alarm bells that had started to appear in recent months. As the water cascaded down my body, I remembered all the forgetful stupid stuff that I had allowed to happen, the lack of focus, the lack of clarity and vision, easily distracted, no motivation, and that overwhelming feeling of being a slave to my To-Do list. Even on this Sunday, a supposed day of rest, I now had to respond to a load of Souterrain emails and prepare a playlist, another To-Do list of sorts, ready for Monday evening's radio show.

I was the one creating the endless lists. I was the one always adding to it. I was giving myself lots of plates to spin, lots of balls to juggle. It came as no surprise that the plates and balls were now beginning to crash to the ground.

The shower gel started to foam around my feet, slowly draining away down the plughole. I'd finished washing minutes earlier. I was now just standing in the shower, hand against the wall, taking deep breaths and looking straight ahead at the grey tiles whilst the deluge of warm water hit the back of my neck. I laughed at the irony of taking a shower whilst worrying about a wet season 5,000 miles away. It was comforting, but very little was going through my mind. I was almost drifting away, soothed by the steady flow of the water. The pump of the shower calibrated itself for a second and the noise shook me out of my trance-like state. I looked down at my fingers and they'd turned to prunes. The wrinkling of my digits was an indication that it was time to get out. No brilliant solutions this time, just a moment to reflect on another thing to add to the growing list.

My walk home from work was so well trodden that I hardly needed to think about the direction or the streets to turn down. I'd neglected this exercise recently and traded it in for a quick train ride home just so I could get started on other Souterrain things that required my overdue attention. I was down a considerable amount of cash after the booking balls-up the day before and payday was not as close as I would have liked so I decided to save whatever I had left by putting one foot in front of the other. It was still something I'd rather have got over with quite quickly, so I walked at pace, while carrying my heavy backpack, looking to get to my end destination in under an hour and fifteen. Sometimes, if I lost interest or found myself going AWOL in my own mind, I would skip the last part of the walk and make a detour to a train station that had no barriers so I could ride one stop for free. I'd yet to be caught by a ticket inspector whenever I'd done it, so I considered rolling the dice again that evening.

The walk had a multi-purpose: I got exercise, I saved money and I could listen to music for an hour or so. Every now and then I needed to make a choice as to whether to overtake someone but other than that my decisions were unconscious. The booking mistake was still playing heavily on my mind and I'd been too embarrassed to talk to anyone about it. Previously, I was impatient, but today I have nothing to do other than put one foot in front of the other, so that mistake rolled around like a pinball in my mind.

I took my iPhone out of my pocket and opened up the FAQ travel document again, zooming in on the content, looking for any way out of the mess I had caused. 'The Journey' by Tom Misch played in my ears, but it had gone from head bopper to background noise, whilst cars simultaneously flashed by on the main road. The aroma from the local fish and chip shop just up ahead was tantalising. A small queue of people were waiting for their battered delights as I peered through the window, envious as I strolled past, slowing my pace a little. On the document, the first line of text quickly blurred into the second and words on the screen become dots as I scrolled upwards looking for something, I don't know what. Being in no state to read, I'd quickly gone from stubbornly solving something myself to a preconceived last resort of calling the airline within a matter of minutes. I begrudgingly typed the numbers into the phone, already convincing myself this was a wasted effort. An automated message greeted me and gave me a number of options to select:

Please press one to make a booking.

Press two if you've already made a booking and would like to discuss current bookings.

Beep.

To my surprise, I was connected to an advisor straight away and I wasn't prepared for any questions he had for me.

"How can I help you, sir?" he asked politely.

I paused due to my pride, feeling tense about sharing my blunder but, on reflection, what this simple call represented was a step away from thinking I had all the answers. It was a swallowing of my pride and asking for help, something I had a fear of because I thought it showed weakness, a chink in the macho perfectionist armour.

"Err, hi, yes, I made an error yesterday in booking a flight and I really need your help to rectify it," I splurt, uncomfortably.

Even me admitting it was my error felt nauseous.

"Of course, sir, that's what we're here for. Let's see what we can do."

Over the next couple of minutes, the helpful advisor talked me through some options, and they were all quite simple ones, but ones I had been blind to because of my over-consumed mind. Sharing the problem and talking it over with this stranger down the phone loosened my tense shoulders.

"We can change the dates for no cost, if that works for you, sir?"

"Really? That's great, let me just look at a few things and call you back," I said excitedly.

Relief flowed through my body as I was presented with a light at the end of a tunnel. That's all I needed for my brain to click back into gear and formulate a plan incorporating the mistake but making it work for us. I felt like I had some control back.

I got straight on the phone to Hayley, even though I was just ten minutes away from home.

"I think we can fix it!" I yelled to her emphatically.

"We have to fly from Slovenia to Myanmar at some point, there's no getting around that, otherwise we forfeit the £733. What about if we flip it all around and go west first, rather than east?

Right then we picked a date in December 2017, a day or so after our US visas would run out, and agreed for that to be our mid-way point, where we would transition from western culture to eastern. The plan was to now find another flight from our friends' August wedding in Slovenia to Canada and then travel into the USA for the remainder of summer and autumn, then go from USA back across to Slovenia for this rearranged flight over to Myanmar and carry on with the trip from there.

"That makes so much more sense to do it that way, why didn't we [meaning me] think of that before?" Hayley responds.

"I don't know!"

Maybe I didn't really know then, but I came to understand a bit later.

My mind was so full of chaos, overwhelmed by mental clutter that simple transactional choices and decisions suddenly became more complex and difficult than they needed to be. I had a never-ending list of jobs to do, or 'shoulds', and in fact you could probably say that I was 'shoulding' all over myself. My ability to think clearly and make decisions, even simple ones like phone someone else for help, was clouded. My brain was fogged. Another explanation of mental clutter that I found a couple of years ago from the Association of Professional Declutterers and Organisers in the UK (APDO), was that striving for perfectionism, and then beating yourself up for failing to achieve it, was a sign of mental clutter. It's something I still work on today, mixed with super-high expectations of myself and a healthy dose of imposter syndrome from time to time.

Letting go of the need to be perfect, to know how to solve everything or to be 'the best', is no easy task. It's probably the hardest part of my journey to date and one that requires most attention. I find it a little easier to adjust my internal dialogue from 'shoulds' to 'coulds' and then decide if, deep down, it really needs to be done. I also like to use an oldie but a goodie: what's the worst that can happen? Generally, then I've found myself to be catastrophising and realise that actually no one else really gives a shit about the thing I'm spending so much mental bandwidth on.

Granted, there will always be niggly little tasks that need to get done and being more intentional about batching them together or making a day of it to get it over with does feel quite satisfying, but now I'd rather be spending my energy in the present and regularly try to filter and flush out the negative.

Coaching definitely helps with this, whether self-coaching or finding someone to verbalise the mental clutter to, I can then sift through all the crap and keep what's valuable, and, guess what, ditch the rest.

Once I got home, I felt like we were back in the game. The catastrophe of losing hundreds of pounds, when cash was tight, was avoided and we had more clarity and direction for the trip. A small bit of structure had appeared in this planning and it felt liberating. Hayley was excited also to tell me of her news as well.

Because the sabbatical option had worked for my career situation, she attempted to replicate that at her workplace. She had recently returned to the media job she had previously walked away from a year or so earlier. The constant nudging and the offer of a less demanding shift pattern convinced her to slip comfortably back into something she was good at, but although she was a familiar face in the building, she was still classed as a new employee. The farcical and bureaucratical red tape meant that only employees that had been at the company for over a certain amount of time would be able to take a career break. Broken service didn't count. Once again caught up in the web of life and stuff outside of her control, she immediately decided that when the time came for us to leave, she would just quit, wrestling back control. To her, and me, this reset was far more important than a job and a few technicalities were not going to get in her way, our way, in making that happen.

PHASE TWO

Let It All Go

"As I declutter and downsize, I gradually discover more of my essence and purpose."
Lisa J. Shultz, *Lighter Living*

5. Clutter

As February 2017 approached, and with six months until our first flight, I felt a need to fill the time and make myself busy. In the back of my mind I knew I should have been dedicating time to figuring out a travel itinerary, researching visas, injections and contemplating the overall cost but the thought of it was just a little too overwhelming. I was looking to be distracted.

One crap job that I'd put off for ages was organising my music. I had purchased tons of .mp3 files that were then on different devices and it was just a matter of time before the old laptop that held the majority of them gave up the ghost. Each day I left them there without backing them up, I ran the risk of losing them all. With all this perceived time to fill, I talked myself into prioritising this boring but necessary task, which was a distraction from having to face the difficult but more important stuff like exercising. I'd had a gym membership for a place around the corner from work, but I'd yet to break a sweat there in the three months since I started giving them money. To get the job done, I devised a simple plan: I made copies of all the song files and transferred them over to an external hard drive. I had a few of them hiding in drawers too, of that I was sure. I could then remove any duplicates and upload them onto the iPad – my primary hub of all my files that we would take away with us. A late addition to the plan was an opportunity to gather up the hundreds of CDs we had accumulated over the years and had just followed us from place to place. We no longer even owned a CD player and hadn't done for several years. I could burn all the discs on to my ropey old laptop and then move the files in with all the others. Perfect. This distraction was loosely connected to our travels, I told myself, because we'll need music to listen to while we're away. There we are, I thought. I had convinced myself it was the right thing to do. Easy.

One hour in and I was smashing through hundreds of downloads and transferring them from one place to another.

I'd corrected typos in song titles and created folders so it was easier for me to sort them. Top-level organisation skills were on display. I stacked up the CD cases next to me and some showed considerable signs of wear and tear. No matter the condition they were in, they had all played a small part in shaping my identity and contributing to my love for music – well, most of them did. I looked quizzically at one or two purchases such as *Punk Goes Crunk*, an awful covers album of punk bands playing rap tracks, and wondered why I had ever spent the money on them. I put them in the laptop and burned them to my master file anyway. Maybe, one day, I would choose to listen to them.

I was in a rhythm now; it was like a little one-man factory set-up. All the CDs waiting to go through the process were on the sofa to my right, all the completed ones were on the floor in a pile to my left, the empty cases and homeless discs were put to one side to deal with later. The disc drive in the laptop was working double time to burn the singles and albums in a matter of seconds and the transfers were moving along at a decent speed. I could feel the warmth of the machine as the fan was kicking out the heat to avoid malfunction, it was trying, but its better days were behind it. Some files required editing due to the rarity of some of the purchases (or copies from someone else) which was fine, I didn't mind labelling (organising again), it felt like a quick achievement, like I was giving myself a future gift of time, everything was where it should have been and I could save precious seconds whilst looking for the right song at the right moment.

The stack to the left of me was growing so I made a mental note to make sure I was careful not to knock them over. I worked at a fast pace and, somehow, started to lose track of where I'd put the last couple of discs. Unsurprisingly, because I was doing multiple things at once, I started to place discs in the wrong pile, and I had to go back and check which ones I'd already done, which set me back twenty minutes. After a quick recap I felt the need for some hydration as I'd been shuffling stuff around for a while. As I leant forward to get up from the comfort of my sofa, my left elbow knocked the stack of CDs and the top half came crashing down, some bouncing against the TV cabinet and scattering all over the floor. I called myself a fucking idiot but at the same time marvelled at how some of them managed to scatter the distance they did. I got on my hands and knees and started to gather them up, letting out a deep sigh of disappointment and aggressively shaking my head. This time, instead of one big pile, I made two smaller ones, which I probably should have done in the first place. Once they were all back in their appropriate stack, I stood up and strolled towards the living room doorway and looked back at my laptop to monitor the progress of the next transfer.

'What did I get up for again?' I thought to myself.

It had literally only been thirty seconds, maybe less, but I needed to stop and go back in time, and it clicked that, yes, I needed a drink.

Fun fact, apparently, this momentary lapse in memory is called the "Doorway Effect" and psychologists believe that passing through a doorway or entering another room creates a mental block in the brain, which means that it resets the memory to make room for the creation of a new episode. Hayley has left her keys in the front door about a dozen times, so I wouldn't be surprised it has something to do with this.

I turned around and headed to the kitchen and with my first footstep in the direction of hydration all I hear is a crack, swiftly followed by a sharp pain. I'd just planted my bare foot into an open CD case and in doing so snapped the hinges and shattered the lid.

"You fucking mug," I shouted as I pointed aggressively at the lifeless case. Because I was on my own, it was acceptable to go full-on Incredible Hulk mixed with Danny Dyer at an inanimate object. That's not weird, is it? If I had a branch close by, I'd have given the case a damn good thrashing like Basil Fawlty did with that Austen 1100. My left foot displayed a small cut and I shook my head in disappointment at myself for not getting the basics right then picked up the remains and put them in the bin. The pain quickly subsided, and I eventually got to my intended destination. Whilst taking a time out, sipping on my glass of water and rubbing my sole, I looked back at the weird conveyor belt set-up I'd created in the living room, viewing it from a different angle: it looked like a disaster zone. There were CDs, wires and crap everywhere and I immediately started to feel uncomfortable. I suppose being in the eye of the storm was the place of most calm so, on the inside of my own conveyor belt, I didn't recognise the carnage.

I walked piles of CDs down the hallway back to their rightful home on the shelves in the second bedroom. The original shelving arrangement was now all messed up and for some reason they didn't all fit anymore. It was as though they'd multiplied on the short walk. I removed the other trinkets and crap from the shelves to make room – paperwork, ornaments and more DVDs were shuffled around so I could squeeze all the CDs back into their spot. I felt like a contestant on *The Crystal Maze*, moving things around to find the right combination so the all-powerful shelf could release a crystal for me and my teammates. I sensed the pressure to solve this puzzle before I became locked in the Aztec Zone. Unfortunately, there were no teammates shouting words of encouragement and there was no Richard O'Brien – or whoever presents it these days – playing harmonica to the cameraman. Instead, all I heard was my own self-deprecation and a realisation that I was getting frustrated as I slowly turned my back on the challenge and released myself from the room.

A closing of the eyes, an exhale, a look up to the ceiling and a shake of the head. I had been triggered. Similar to the other day with my travel planning spreadsheet, my enthusiasm and motivation for organising had left me. I walked out the spare room, neglecting some CD singles which I had left on the floor, and paced straight to my phone to take my mind off all the junk strewn everywhere.

I scrolled through all my apps looking for an escape, a respite, a brief change of scenery that would take me away from my current location. Nothing interesting was happening on Facebook – does it ever? – and there was not much to engage with on Twitter. I'd already seen those pictures on Instagram. I refreshed my Twitter feed again, thinking maybe I'd missed something interesting from ten seconds prior. At that time, there were about ninety apps on my iPhone, all in a jumble and in no way arranged logically. I probably wasted a few minutes every day just searching for apps. I didn't even use two thirds of them, but I thought they could be useful one day, so I kept them. Right then, I was looking for any one of them to jump out and help me disconnect from my immediate reality, but nothing gave me what I needed. I swiped left on my home screen to spot a few stragglers that I'd not managed to organise yet, thinking I must have downloaded them a while back and since forgotten why. I thought maybe if I moved a few more things around I might feel a sense of achievement?

Groupon was the first app that caught my eye. I'd heard other people's stories of getting good deals on experiences through them, so of course I wanted to be closer to the opportunity of spending more money. The logo was a cool shade of green so I could set it near the Gumtree app (another place to buy stuff). I held down the app until it started to wobble and moved it into position. Skype was another one I hadn't used, but this was in a lighter blue shade. I took the same action and shuffled it near Twitter. The final app that needed moving was Music Magpie. I'd downloaded this months ago before moving back from Brighton, with the intention of selling some duplicate films that Hayley and I both owned. I hadn't noticed we had the same DVDs before, only whilst packing to move to Brighton had I spotted them.

You can never have too many copies of *Napoleon Dynamite* though, I suppose.

Although I made the first step in exploring the removal of the doubles, I never followed through with anything. I opened Music Magpie and its simple layout gave me two options, sell or shop. I hit sell just to see what happened and it asked me what stuff

I wanted to part with. I selected the option of 'CDs, DVDs, books and games' and the screen transformed into a mesmerising block with a single red horizontal line moving up and down immediately searching for a barcode to scan. With this one inadvertent discovery, I once again felt empowered and intrigued. I took a look at the ridiculous towers of CDs I had created and added a new task to the To-Do list.

In this moment, a surge of energised activity hit me. I could do this, I thought. It was time for some of this shit to go.

Moments later, I was a man possessed. If I sold off some of the duplicates, the rest of the stuff would fit nicely on the shelf, I thought to myself, thinking short term. The few duplicates were all scanned into the app but then I quickly got stuck. To sell your items, they had to reach at least a £5 threshold otherwise it was clearly not worth their time to process them. I was a pound short and this pause generated a memory flash at reaching this point last time and stopping, or giving up.

I hunted around looking to scan anything else that could take me over that threshold. I eventually found some books that I had no intention of ever reading. Those additional items put me over the minimum requirement, and I was then up to a massive £5.79. I'm in, I thought. I got that sense of achievement that I was looking for and alongside that, I took pleasure in watching the numbers – money in my pocket – go up.

I was hooked. But I needed another fix.

With my phone in my hand, I transformed into Terminator, scanning the room for anything that had a barcode on it. Nothing was out of bounds as I quickly retrieved handfuls of items from various rooms around the flat and placed them around me in the living room, enclosing myself in a self-made prison of media purchases and gifts from the past twenty years. I had set up another conveyor belt system and attempted to take the first step in letting go of some of my stuff. With all the giddy excitement, I overlooked all of the emotional attachment and sentimental value I had placed on most of the films and games. I thought it was going to be easy, but I immediately found myself struggling. *The Godfather Trilogy, Scarface, The Karate Kid, Ghostbusters, The Sopranos* boxset, all eight seasons (and one average feature film) of the *24* franchise were just a handful of the things that had provided amazing experiences and great enjoyment in the past. I had also either invested a considerable amount of time and money on those things. *24* alone I probably sat through the whole eight seasons at least twice, maybe three times, counting Jack Bauer's incredible body count. I had no idea how much I'd spent on this entertainment, but it would have been in or around the twelve or thirteen-grand mark over a ten-year period considering the volume of stuff that was in front of me.

But now it was time for the stuff to pay me back. Most of it had served its purpose, and some of it hadn't.

I scanned everything. The reality hit me. The expense of these once-lauded items was now next to nothing. My perception of their value versus the actual value in the real world was equivalent to night and day. What did it mean if I was to sell these things for a pittance, basically giving them away? Did it mean that I was not a big enough fan? Did it mean that I was ungrateful? What would happen if, one day, I wanted to watch one of these films, read one of these books or play one of these games? I'd be stuck and I would curse the fact that I traded them in for so little. And then I'd no doubt buy them all over again. What about all the money I'd invested into these things that were mine, that I owned? Surely, I shouldn't just discard them, I thought.

This shiny new task all of a sudden became very uncomfortable. This stuff formed part of my identity. It had shaped a large part of who I was. I wondered whether relinquishing those items would mean I'd be abandoning part of who I was.

I noticed myself clinging on to DVDs that I had never even made the effort to watch. I gave myself false excuses not to sell them. Weirdly, I suddenly noticed I became interested in films that ten minutes earlier I couldn't have given a shit about or even knew were there. Now, they were the most important thing in the world. All of a sudden, I needed them. Hearing the snap of the boxes open as I checked the discs were still in place increased my feelings of ownership. The shimmer of the cellophane wrapping bouncing off the sunlight through the window transformed a once-rejected item into a new shiny gift, ready to be unwrapped. This behaviour was an interesting turn of events that I hadn't anticipated, but I carried on and continued to scan them in anyway, just to see if there were any rarities in the mix. From that point on, every decision I made was even more difficult. I reminded myself of Frodo Baggins, and the One Ring. I so very much wanted to get rid of this mountain of DVDs, and yet they were my precious. To make it easier on myself, I scanned my *Lord of the Rings* DVD and set it aside, carefully. I then tackled the films I had less feeling towards, such as those that were just plain awful, like the 1999 version of *The Mod Squad*. I reminded myself that any additional funds would go towards our travelling, so there lay the carrot, the reason. The why. By reminding myself of the purpose for all this jettisoning, the motivation to stick with it, for at least a little bit, remained.

Day quickly turned to night and the darkness of the room shrouded me in shadow with the only spotlight being the white glow of the redundant iTunes screen from my laptop. I had no concept of time and all the file transfers had finished hours ago. I had not eaten since breakfast, but I was in the zone and that had carried me into the early evening. My original task was complete, but my energy had shifted elsewhere.

Hayley walked in from work to find me sitting on the floor in the middle of the dark living room surrounded by stacks of books, computer games, CDs and DVDs. I had built three main piles of stuff, each with a bit of paper beside it indicating which second-hand retailer they were going to. Next to them was a less-curated heap of things that none of the reselling companies wanted to purchase (it was either a product so mass-produced that they had too many of them already, say *CSI*, or an offering so niche they had no desire for it). They didn't even want them for free.

"What on earth are you doing?" Hayley quizzed as she switched the light on, revealing a tired and hangry version of myself.

"I'm selling it all!" I responded enthusiastically with my hands in the air, very aware that I'd not engaged with another human all day.

"It's not huge, about £165."

"But it's all of your stuff, love," she added, concerned I'd perhaps lost my mind.

"I know, but I never use any of it anymore."

I picked up the *Hamlyn Book of Football Techniques and Tactics* to illustrate my point. "When was the last time I read this?" pointing at a picture of players and artwork from 1989.

Hayley nodded. "Sell it."

I shuffled each Jenga-like tower of books, games, CDs and DVDs slowly out of the living room and into the hallway, making sure not to get too hasty and have the whole thing come crashing down around my bare feet. Again. Carefully lined-up against the wall was a real-life display of a timeline of entertainment and interests that had come and gone. A complex patchwork of different periods of my adult and teenage life all stacked up waiting to be moved on. I'd been living in this flat for a decade and the majority of these things had too. I looked longingly down on the stacks like I was saying goodbye to an old friend, never to be seen again. But then I quickly snapped out of the sentiment and realised I could just as easily watch that old friend on Netflix or one of our other five streaming services that we were paying for.

Within a few days, the 482 (!) items (yes, I went back on the websites and counted) were boxed up and either collected by courier or dropped off at designated pick-up points. Seventy-two hours following that, my bank account was credited with £164.30. Some CD singles I sold for as little as 5p, like Destiny's Child's 'Bills, Bills, Bills', which I bought as an import for a fiver from HMV, because imports didn't get official UK releases until the week after. Some of the bigger-ticket items, if you can call them that, were weird niche books and DVDs that I didn't even know we had. The film *Mobsters* starring Christian Slater went for £5.08 and a DVD called *The Secret Life of Elephants* went for £6. I don't recall watching either. Years of decisions, collections, accumulations and a considerable part of my identity had gone in a matter of days. In truth, I probably went a bit overboard with trying to squeeze the optimal amount of money from the different buy-back apps (sometimes the difference in price was pennies) but reflecting back, it was a great exercise and a bit of a wake-up call to really see the actual monetary value of my things rather than the perceived value that ownership had led me to believe. I also enjoyed the trip down memory lane that going through the DVDs and CDs allowed me. Sometimes, I baffled myself with stuff I had no recollection of obtaining and there were a few 'what the fuck was I thinking' moments, but it was nice to briefly attach a memory to a film, or a game. It made me realise that my attachment to these physical items was ultimately redundant. And, besides, I was now looking to the future ahead, not the past behind.

The days that followed were different. I felt lighter. More in control. The living room appeared fresher, cleaner even. Part of the unit looked bare, sparse, almost longing to be utilised again. On display were only my most favourite films and books, the best of the best, about 10 per cent of what was there only a few days ago.

Even though I hadn't really been aware of what I had done, I didn't want this whole experiment to be attributed to being without. I didn't want the place to be void of things, it was never about suffering or starving myself of items, so keeping those last few pieces of entertainment that added the most value made complete sense to me. The empty spaces on the shelves threatened me to fill them with shiny new objects and it was difficult to deny the temptation, especially knowing that a new display of things was a mere few clicks away. My world view had now shifted, even if just a little. I waited for the feelings of guilt and regret to kick in for abandoning many of my belongings but, you know what? They never came.

With my minimalist mindset like it is now, I don't necessarily need a huge purge like this often. Looking back, it was very cathartic, being able to act in the moment whilst being with my stuff. Because I find the action part so simple (the emotional attachment, sentimental value and endowment effect parts are trickier, of course), taking something off a hanger and putting it in a bag, there will be regular intervals during the year where a trip to the dump or charity shop is required and that's OK, it's just part of my continued maintenance. If I don't bring shit into my world, I don't have to deal with it.

6. Too Many Clothes

Once out the other side of the entertainment decluttering, I started sharing the details of my less-than-exciting weekend – I told Hayley I called it 'The Purge' – with any fucker who would listen. I rang my brother who I hadn't spoken to in a couple of weeks and told him how much of my stuff I'd sold. I annoyingly tried to convince work colleagues to offload their DVDs so they could feel the same smug way I did. Friends, family, anyone who showed the slightest bit of interest in the weekend purge, received an excitable monologue of how good it felt to relinquish the things that surrounded me.

Unsurprisingly, my hysteria in flogging a load of old crap didn't interest anyone as much as it did me and I received more questioning looks than reassuring pats on the back. Why would they not want to feel this way, I thought to myself. I was still on a 'shoppers high', but in reverse. The truth was that this purge was uneventful for most… but, to me, it felt like the start of something. Genuinely. It felt good, and that was a feeling I wanted to chase after again.

Financially, things were starting to look up a little too. The sale of the DVDs was just the start of a two-week window where random sums of money landed in my account. Pay-outs from venues for Souterrain music nights, DJ sets and offers of compensation following a series of complaints (remember Southern Fail?) all made their way back to me. Those additions just added momentum to the goal of getting out of debt and saving more money for travelling. We'd also booked another flight, in the right direction this time, from Ljubljana, leaving all our friends at the August wedding to go over to Toronto and start the Canadian part of the tour. Further bookings had to wait for the time being. Still on a high from seeing our living space with less, I realised that within the flat was potentially a load more stuff that could be jettisoned for cash. Items that could be a bargain and valuable to someone else and help build our savings.

Next Saturday, and feeling energised from the previous week's purge, I wandered into the second bedroom, scanning it again Terminator-style for unused items. The sofa bed was like a tractor beam, pulling me towards it. Within its excessive three storage drawers were a number of Hayley's things that I knew hadn't been used in a while. The middle drawer required some forceful manipulation to open but hidden to the rear was a digital camera safely stored in a discoloured box. The corners of the packaging had softened and no longer matched the original red tint. Sellotape on each side flapped around loose, its years of stickiness long behind it.

"Do you want to keep this camera?" I asked Hayley, hoping that the answer was "no" but remaining aware it belonged to her.

Hayley had forgotten it was even there but was non-committal. "I'm not sure, let me have a look at it."

Alongside the camera, stored in another drawer, was a torn box full of other video and photography equipment, an accumulation of digital point-and-shoot gear. While I left her to go through it all, I made my way down the hall into the main bedroom to take a look at some of the clothes I'd not worn in ages.

If I thought the DVDs were tricky to let go of, my clothes were another level. I took pride in my appearance, I'm not ashamed to say that. I'd bought a lot of clothes over the years, mainly high-street fast fashion mixed with items that were quirky and stood out. But I had favourites. I knew I did, so I opened the wardrobe and pulled out all the hangers, some of which had two or three shirts or t-shirts on them, and threw everything on the bed. I squeezed through to get to the box of sports gear and accessories and threw the contents of that on top of the pile. From the kitchen I grabbed five plastic bags, each displaying a different shop or supermarket, from a drawer that has been specifically designated to contain all the plastic bags. Do you have one of those? Pulling one drawer out, you got another one free. It didn't close properly because of the overflow but I swaggered back into the bedroom and threw the bags on the floor. I can do this, I thought. A little space was left on the bed by the headboard, so I took my place next to this huge pile and got my phone out. A job like this needed a soundtrack so I shuffled the N*E*R*D album *In Search of...* and to my delight, 'Lapdance' kicked in and I got to work.

I targeted the sports gear first as that was what had landed on top of the pile and there were several things that got put into the first plastic bag – destined for charity. Or the recycling centre. Old sweat bands were tossed, one so discoloured that it barely resembled its original shade of white. Football kits from local teams and five-a-side games that I had not worn or seen in ages. At this stage, I didn't really know what I was going to do with the contents, but it needed to be removed from where it currently resided. A couple of pairs of football shorts were added, one of them looked like it had the resemblance of a blood stain on it. I would take a few knocks most five-a-side games attempting to nutmeg people and in retaliation they would barge me into the boards that surrounded the 3G pitches. Golf tees, balls, scorecards and a cover for a driver I no longer owned were all thrown into the bags. There was no sentiment, I felt detached from it all. Rolled up in balls and misshapen were several Chelsea shirts... and there was the moment I paused... and my good form was stopped dead in its tracks. With a tender hand, I opened out each one of the kits and laid them proudly on the bed. Out of respect. Dozens of shirts from seasons past all held memories of my own fun playing in matches with friends, winning important games, losing silly ones, training sessions, arguments, hugs, laughs... everything, was in those tops. The shirts also showed my support for the club over the years and half of them had players names on the back from recent eras. Hasselbaink, Di Matteo, Hazard, Lampard, Terry, J. Cole, Poyet, Morris, Gullit, Stein, Hoddle, Drogba, Essien. Legends, and some of my all-time favourite players. I used to wear those shirts when going to Stamford Bridge and on away days to see them play. The Hasselbaink shirt had a small rip in the left shoulder after my mate Mark jumped on me as we went mad after a Frank Lampard ninety-sixth minute winner against Stoke. He must have caught his watch in the material or something, but we couldn't put our finger on how it happened. We'd sat next to the away fans and we got nothing but abuse from fat old white blokes all game, and then they took the lead on the hour. When Frank's goal went in down our end, we gave them a load of shit back. That was a crazy ten seconds.

I also used to wear them in social situations to be part of a community, to show my true colours, so to speak. I haven't felt the need to show off my passion or desire for the club in a while, so they've not been worn. My support didn't fade, but I no longer needed to publicly display my affiliation, especially as the cost of each additional season's home, away and third shirt would take a large chunk out of my wages. Mixed in with the Chelsea shirts were a number of others I had collected over the years: a Dutch national shirt from the 1998 World Cup, a Lille white away shirt from my trip to France, a Napoli shirt from 1995, a gift from a distant Italian cousin, and a Tunisia national shirt from 2009. Chelsea training tops and unofficial title-winning t-shirts were unfolded too. I was surprised to see some of them again as I thought they had been lost in kit bags or left in sweaty changing rooms.

I wore each of these kits whilst playing so each one held a version of my more athletic days, a younger, fitter me that wouldn't be impacted physically by playing football three or four times a week. Although I hadn't played for a few years, every now and then I would long to kick a ball about, maybe not in the settings or the intensity of the past, but sometimes I missed it. If I was to discard the kits, I thought I'd be fully shutting the door on any type of return. Whether it was true or not, that's what was at stake. Here it was again, the emotional attachment. Knocking on my door like an unwelcome neighbour. Rather than deal with it head on and question whether they still served a purpose, I left the kits to one side. I wasn't ready to let go of the chance of playing football again and the kits still represented that option. And, besides, I wasn't trying to impress anyone with my organisation.

I could go at my speed.

Conscious that I was still making some sort of progress, I shifted my focus back to the pile of other clothes and aimed to just reduce volume and not to completely discard everything. If I filled some bags and generally had less than when I started, then I'd be happy with that, I thought. With my own expectations set, I felt able to carry on focusing on the aim of less and not getting too hung up on what I didn't get rid of.

Down the years, the behaviour and habits associated with these clothes had driven a reputation and certain labels to be attached to me. I would generally be late to most events because of never being quite satisfied with the outfit I had selected for the day or evening. My friends would expect me to turn up late. They would often tell me wrong times so I would turn up at the same time everyone else did. Even for work, I would turn up later than normal. Hardly an attitude that endears you to bosses. The predicament I put myself in on a daily basis would lead people to think that I didn't care, or it wasn't important enough for me to show up on time. The truth of the matter was always that I just tangled myself up in knots about how I looked, and which type of shirt went with which pair of jeans. Hours were lost in making decisions on which arrangement was best for the day, but most of the time I never really felt settled. It may have sounded all very trivial to some, but it mattered to me.

A couple of V-necks were placed in the bag, swiftly followed by a black long-sleeve top I forgot I even had. A few jumpers, some office attire, white shirts with buttons missing, they all got analysed, inspected, then folded up and placed in a bag. Ill-fitting casual shirts once loved were discarded, one even had a massive hole in the armpit. How long that had been there for, I wondered. Ripped jeans with more rip than jean padded out a couple more bags. As I held each item, and for a moment reconnected with it, I could almost talk myself into holding on to it. I created scenarios – fantasies – in my head where the item of clothing I was holding featured as the special guest star. If I ever wanted to go to a fancy-dress party as Joey from *Friends* when he wore everything Chandler owned, I'd have plenty to choose from. The words "just in case" rattled around my head on repeat. Three simple words that were becoming more prominent as each day went by. "Just in case", was a simple saying not too long ago that hardly had any connotation to it. It was the low-risk safety net, almost like a get-out clause to avoid making any difficult decisions. I said it all the time, but I never thought those words could present themselves as a blocker from moving on. However I framed it, "I might need it someday," or "You never know, it might come in handy," just highlighted a deeper fear of missing out. FOMO. The fear that if I let something go, I'd potentially miss out on a great experience or have to pay again for something I already owned, which would then have made me feel inadequate or stupid for getting rid of it in the first place. Just in case I ever wanted to wear that KISS t-shirt with glitter on it I'd have it ready to go. Positive and negative scenarios popped up in my head to try and convince me it would be wrong to pass on these items to someone else. That building feeling of loss made me hesitant. It generated an awkwardness where conflict was on the horizon. Being an introvert, conflict was – and sometimes still is – something I tried to avoid at all costs. The conflict was internal and, because of all the accumulation of stuff over the years, I saw that I was losing more physical things than I was gaining. I was throwing good money away, I kept thinking – falsely. Letting go of my clothes felt like a tragedy because I couldn't initially see what I gained out of discarding them. I wasn't replacing them. I'd had a wave of motivation and felt a little lighter seeing the entertainment go so that was something to cling on to; the money certainly helped but that was not an option here. It felt uncomfortable, wrong even, but at least I felt something. The clothes were no longer just hidden from view. They were in my line of sight, and I could decide what happened to them: judge, jury and executioner. Or redeemer?

I reminded myself of the whole point in this purging, which often got lost in all the memories and decision fatigue. I was not going to take all these things travelling with me, I thought, and I did not want to burden my friends and family by having them store all my crap in their homes, which is what we considered doing. I certainly did not want to pay for any storage because, honestly, we couldn't afford it. The fact that this was feeling uncomfortable was a good thing and was another example of how just letting go of the past a little and moving on felt like the right thing to do. As I have come to learn, the great thing about the past is you always know where it is, should you need to go back to it.

All five bags were now full of clothing and accessories. Bracelets, cheap jewellery and broken watches sprinkled themselves amongst poor purchasing decisions, stuff that no longer fit and sections of a wardrobe that had not been visited for a considerable amount of time. As I rummaged around the back of the wardrobe like some lost member of the Pevensie family, I reminisced about the time I spent more than $300 (£225) in a Manhattan Armani store on a cream jumper that never fit. That jumper sat at the top of the pile, taunting me, because I was never going to get that money back and it knew it. That was a sunk cost and I had to just swallow that. Most of the items were still in good condition but they had been superseded over time by other preferences, my "go-to" items. I'd say probably only 30 per cent of my wardrobe was used regularly. Only a few of the items in the bags were likely to hold any monetary value so there was little financial benefit for me in doing this. But if I could donate the items then it would benefit others. The bags got lined up out in the hallway where the stacks of DVDs lay abandoned just a few days prior. That area of the hallway had become like the twilight zone, whatever got put there vanished in a matter of days. I left the remaining clothing on the bed to put back in the wardrobe and walked back down the hall into the second bedroom to see Hayley sat on the floor surrounded by paperwork and boxes.

"I've put those two cameras on eBay," she informed me.

"Two!?"

"Yeah, there was another digital camera in one of the boxes, so I've put them both on eBay."

"Oh, wow, nice one."

"I've also got loads of old paperwork and contracts from jobs that I need to throw out but I'm not doing that today," she added. Letting go of those cameras was enough for now, she surmised.

The wardrobe and drawers still looked full but less so, and right then I was comfortable that less was progress. And less is still progress now. I acknowledged the strange sensations of loss and feeling uncomfortable but having that many clothes was just not practical. Plus, I couldn't take them all away with me, anyway. To have "options" was always my excuse for holding on to all those items, but without knowing it, I was only selecting from a preferred range anyway.

The rest were just... passengers.

7. Questions

The fast-paced sound of taps on keyboards and general busy-ness filled the Croydon office. The intricate balance of people quietly engrossed in whatever they were doing was momentarily dashed by the crash of the door and heavy stomping footsteps as colleagues wandered behind me. The noise of mid-week peak productivity reverberated around my workspace while I sat quietly, pen behind my ear, staring at the scaffolding wrapped around a half-built block of flats out the window. Someone was printing loads of pages a couple of feet away; I felt their presence behind me as they stared over my shoulder at one of the two large TVs mounted on the wall whilst waiting for their printer job to finish. Sky News was on but no sound emerged from the TV, however the subtitles flickered relentlessly. Whilst the printer's beeps added to the sensory cacophony, I instinctively reacted by rearranging my relaxed seated position, a position I'd had for years, and folded my right leg underneath me. I'd never sat like this before. It was a different reaction and it felt a little strange. I was becoming more aware and sensitive to annoyances and distractions around me. Before I wouldn't have even noticed things like this, lost in boredom and treading water in a sea of tasks.

Different habits were starting to take shape. I was waking up twenty minutes earlier, I was getting an earlier train to work, I wasn't rushing around as much and this whole new seated position was another one I'd noticed. My standard, everyday position of sitting in front of multiple screens was comfortable. Sometimes, I even took my shoes off under the desk. I saw the same information from the same angle every day and that kept me on autopilot. I didn't need to think too much, so I didn't. The slight annoyance of distracting noise around me caused a twitch and this new quirk made me sit differently. My default position was to get the office chair as low as possible and slouch, looking so laid back that it might have been conceived that I couldn't give a shit. That genuinely wasn't the case, more comfortable you could say, complacent, maybe. This new awkward kink in the line changed the angle of how I saw my screens (yes, I needed two) and simultaneously I changed the angle of how I viewed a lot of things. My outlook was looking a little clearer at home and that replicated itself mentally. The less physical objects that surrounded me all of a sudden made it easier to be more aware of my surroundings. I felt less congested. There was suddenly a space that I didn't feel compelled to fill. It's as though the clearing of the material clutter was a visual representation of what was now going on inside my head: a spring clean, of sorts.

There was still stuff to do to reach the goal of being debt free, increase savings and then travel without financial guilt but the path felt less obstructed. I was having more stints of focus and moments of flow, even though the elements around me teased me with distraction. Each item, belonging, or thing I owned was like a small obstacle in my way; the more items I removed, the clearer the road became. I had realised that my belongings, my habits, were my safety net. By cutting away the net I felt exposed and vulnerable, but it was also very freeing. And necessary. Not just from a practical perspective – I needed the money – but from a personal perspective too – I felt unburdened. As if I had grown as a person. At the age of thirty-five had I finally turned into a mature adult? Or was this something more?

I also found myself with a little bit more time. The once cold blocks that needed to be filled were, in the main, still being filled, but with more thought behind them. My lunch times at work, once locked up creating endless and probably pointless online events on random websites for Souterrain were now replaced by going for a walk or going to the gym. As it was only a five-minute walk away from the office, there were no more excuses not to go and work out. So, every Tuesday and Thursday I would take a later lunch, to let the rush pass, and then swing over, do forty minutes' worth of weights and then go back to work. On Wednesdays, once I'd finished for the day, I would pop in there and run a cheeky five kilometres, get on the rowing machine for ten minutes and then finish off on the bike. It wasn't excessive but it was consistent. I'd then get the train home and still be back at roughly the same time as if I was to walk all the way, which I started to do more of on the rest of the evenings. It was like I was training for travel and because I had that 'why' it gave me motivation to get myself into good shape. Plus, I fancied tackling one of the *Man vs Food* challenges at a back-street American diner.

For the next three months or so, Hayley and I continued to jettison items from the flat. About three months before we set off on our travels, the decluttering of our flat led me to really question a lot of things that were in my control and sphere of influence. Through listening to others around me, I unlocked some knowledge that was already in my head somewhere but never referred to. I'd heard but never listened. What could I control and what could I influence? Once those things were clear and understood, I could then decide to do something about them. I could control how I responded to challenges or obstacles, my mindset, self-talk and what I consumed. The rest of the stuff that was out of my control, such as other people's reactions or perceptions, the weather and Southern Fail, I couldn't affect, so why spend the time or energy worrying about it? Easier said than done, I thought, but I had started to recognise moments of frustration about things I had no control over. I let them go.

It was during this countdown to our travelling that I also noticed other personality traits take over. By clearing my headspace, it allowed new emotions, new ideas, to pop in. I first noticed I regressed back to feeling like a beginner or having an almost child-like inquisitive behaviour. I found myself asking "why?" on a daily basis. To everything. I questioned all that I saw. I was waking up to the realisation that I had drifted along rather than play an active role in the design of my life. Even my outlook at work shifted a little. I became increasingly aware of the time my team was spending on work that was, quite frankly, unnecessary. Time spent on lengthy reports that no one read, meetings for the sake of meetings, wasting the time and skills of these highly intelligent and experienced people. I also started to notice the number of items that were duplicated, requested but never followed up, or work To-Do's that were not needed in the first place. Every work item my team and I received was labelled as "urgent" and "top priority" and "needed to be done yesterday", and yet it really didn't need to be done at all. Having buried my head in the sand for so many years drifting along, wanting to look busy and be busy, I was completely blind to how much time we all wasted doing shit that never really mattered. It was a smokescreen. I noticed, in particular, how this especially applied to me. I'd been going to the same fruitless meetings (that lasted for hours) where nothing ever happened. I'd talked to the same people about the same thing over and over and over again without moving forward. And that continual circular discussion had delayed or blocked a new idea or a new piece of work from ever materialising. We were in a holding pattern. As someone much cleverer than I once said, doing the same over and over again and expecting different results is the definition of insanity.

I had become too worried about what the negative consequences of changing the pattern might have brought rather than the positives it could bring. The self-inflicted red tape had started to frustrate me to the core. Everyone around me had focused on the volume of stuff being completed, not the quality. At work, more meant better. But it was a falsehood. More doesn't mean better. It meant busier. And busier meant qualifying your salary, your worth. So, the notion went unchallenged – because no company is going to pay you more for doing less, unless I, we, can do something about that. I noticed that at my company employees were praised and rewarded for how busy they were or how hard they worked, and challenged and interrogated if they ever implied you had less to do. Busyness syndrome, I think, or boondoggling, doing low-value work to look busy. So, work just kept getting piled on other work. And, like the stacks of CDs in my living room, eventually it was going to come crashing down.

My team was pressured to complete work to tight timescales

only for stakeholders, who were nowhere near ready to receive it, just to sit on it. I started to see the lost hours of productivity by highly paid and highly skilled people doing things that were not particularly powerful or progressive.

So, on one particular Tuesday, I decided to see what would happen if I just stopped doing a particular task that I'd been doing on and off for about six months. I had to put together a bunch of random rules and scores to, apparently, highlight which insurance product was more or less susceptible to the risk of fraud based on staff training and system controls. I can't even remember how I got roped into doing it but I'm sure a decision maker somewhere mentioned it would be good to put together, just in case. I'd spent ages collecting information and putting it all in a fancy-coloured spreadsheet.

Fuck me, I'm boring myself even writing it.

I spent hours talking to people, getting access to different systems I didn't need, just to "check them out", reformat an ever increasing Excel database and then add commentary and recommendations to it. No one fucking read it or was interested in what it was. I remember trying to set up several meetings about it with the person whose idea it was in the first place to see what else they wanted but every single one got swerved. Weeks went by and no one asked about it. Weeks then turned into months and it had all been forgotten about. It turned out, nothing happened once I stopped working on it. It got lost in a directory somewhere, saved in some folder that was never looked at. That leader had moved on months before and their fickle mind had flitted onto something else, so I learnt from that moment to see through the momentary excitement of others and swat away other people's 'shoulds' as well as my own.

"What could you be doing if you didn't have to do this?" I asked Jules, one of the team, whilst pointing at a stack of folders on her desk. I left her to ponder the response.

What was I wasting my time on that could be better spent elsewhere, I challenged myself as I noticed the banner of a new flurry of emails flash up and then quickly disappear.

I had a stack of things to do at work, with Souterrain and at home so I grabbed a few minutes just to re-organise my thoughts. My mental 'To-Do' list was overrun with stuff which previously would have been given some sort of order. These things would have been organised and allocated time and energy to complete. On that day, my 'why' took over. Each thing I thought about, I asked why I'd chosen to do that thing and why I deemed it so important. I had spent hours setting up online events on various platforms telling people about the next Souterrain gig, but I genuinely didn't know how much difference it made. Why did I keep doing it? Music was, and will always be, I hope, a passion of mine but all this superfluous stuff I did around the edges was destroying that passion. Souterrain was a passion project but what would happen when the passion fell out of that sentence?

My train of thought had no light at the end of the tunnel on this occasion, so I stopped thinking about how anxious it all made me feel. I had a meeting to attend shortly, though I couldn't remember what the purpose of me going was, so it couldn't be that important, right?

Now would probably be a good time to remind you of that stat you read way back in the introduction. "Employees ranked meaningless tasks as their number one factor from keeping them feeling fulfilled at work. The vast majority of an employee's day (60 per cent) is wasted on excessive emails, unproductive meetings and a lack of standard process and collaboration."

According to Jason Fried in his book *It Doesn't Have to Be Crazy at Work*, one of my faves by the way, meetings should be used as a last resort and time and attention should be your most valuable resource. Here's one to ponder on. Have you got a meeting coming up soon? Do you really need to be there? Could it be done in half the time? Does it even need to take place at all?

I wandered through my own mind, unlocking boxes of knowledge and suppressed challenges that had been packed away in the back of cupboards. In those boxes were more questions and I started to empty them out all over the place.

What was blocking me from achieving what I wanted to achieve?
What did I even want to achieve?
What did I value?
What were my values?
Did what I do align with the person I wanted to be?
Who was I?

Bloody hell, I thought to myself. This became philosophical pretty quickly. But the real facts were that I didn't know the answers to many of those questions. I'd been so caught up in getting on with life that I had let it get away from me. I had no values anymore.

The reason why I kept doing hundreds of things all at the same time was because I didn't know which of those things aligned with who I wanted to be and what I wanted to do. I valued everything and nothing at the same time, so when I asked myself if this thing added value to my life, my answer was always something like, "maybe". Followed by a mental shrug. That's the other reason why I had kept – hoarded – stuff and why I kept ploughing away doing lots of things, but not actually going anywhere. The things held me down, and I was effectively treading water just to stay afloat. I'd likely adopted some sort of patchwork value-based system from a variety of different places and people that I wasn't aware of and then started to build my decisions and actions around that. Maybe I tagged on bits from my family, my friends, the industry I worked in, the leaders I looked up to (and the ones I didn't) and the music community I had found myself in, but I didn't really know.

I really needed to take some time to think about this a lot more, I concluded. Money and status felt right a decade ago. But, in that moment, life had moved on, and I wasn't so sure anymore.

A physical response to this was to close down a bunch of different databases and Microsoft Office tabs I had open on one of my screens. Next, I opened my top drawer. Naturally, a bunch of pens and paper clips flew out. I gathered up all the stationery and offered it out to the team, checking if anyone else had any need for another four, slightly chewed pens. Most of the junk was put back in the stationery cupboard for someone else to use or recycled where possible. All this existential thinking had jolted me up out of my seat. I mindlessly walked over to the section of the large filing cabinet my team had been allocated and just began to pull out huge binders filled with paperwork and stacked them on an empty desk. There were folders for staff who had left years ago mixed in with wild abandoned and out-of-date training documents. All of it useless. I pulled them all out of their plastic sheaths and put them in the confidential waste bin.

This was the first small step.

It was definitely not the most important or valuable thing I could have been doing at that moment but I felt I needed to copy the purge I'd just done at home, this time at work, and to try and replicate that clarity.

And then it hit me.

I remember the moment quite vividly. I was holding a black folder full of 'important' information from 2009.

I don't want this anymore, I thought.

I don't want to be here.

I needed to let this job go.

Because if I didn't do something about it soon, like my stuff, my career would take ownership of me and it would never let me go.

For my own growth, I needed to get away – move forward – and do something different that aligned with values that I wanted, needed, to re-discover. I wanted to know what it felt like to be the new guy again; I wanted to be able to craft my own way from scratch. I wanted to be able to make a difference. I wanted to be more creative. I needed meaningful work. New values I'm sure would form over time but I worried that if I stayed in that job for much longer, I'd end up with a collection of what ifs and deflated loyalty balloons. I had taken my foot off the accelerator. But now I just felt the need to drive. Anywhere.

I spent the next two and a half hours or so randomly

decluttering my workstation and nearby cabinets. I texted Hayley. In that moment, a thought filled my consciousness.

"Let's sell the flat," I said like a man possessed – but not of his possessions.

"Let's do it!" she responded without missing a beat.

8. No Keys

Three months later the flat was empty. What was once a cluttered living space was now a blank canvas. The rays of mid-morning summer sun forced their way through the large trees and unkempt foliage outside the living room window onto the wiped-down walls and steam-cleaned carpeted floor. The light split the space in two making it look fresh and inviting. Dust particles floated alongside the rays providing a slight haze as they bounced off the closed blinds. Areas of cream carpet previously hidden by dark drawers and storage units now appeared more vibrant than the rest. The slight indentations of home living mapped out our previous furniture arrangement and intersected with small lighter spots which were only visible to the trained eye. The bleached spots sprinkled mainly around the previous seated area highlighted instances of hilarious blunders. As I look proudly around the super-clean flat, memories came flooding back of the time that Hayley spilled hot gravy down herself and then threw it up the wall, all over the sofa and the floor. I supposed that's what you deserve when you try and fill up your plate with too much KFC and then place that plate on a cushion as you climb onto the sofa quickly in order to shotgun the corner spot, the most comfortable of nooks. That comical error will stand the test of time. It remains the most ridiculous and outrageous spillage I have ever seen.

Our much-loved L-shaped sofa with footstool doubled up as an extension to the lounge space. We removed the feet to make the whole thing about a foot lower. If you wanted to relax in our home, you had to fall into it. My parents complained every time they visited because it was so low, they struggled to get up. My dad would sit on the edge, so his feet were still touching the floor. My mum would perch herself uncomfortably at the other end. The brown corduroy upholstery and leather arms were the base for a decade of chilling; this sofa would swallow you up for hours and spit you out all dishevelled. You really had to give yourself up to the thing because once you were there, it would have to take something pretty important to get up off it.

The time and effort spent on repainting the whole place before we left had definitely been worth it, however it's not something I planned to do again anytime soon. The clean and bright white vibes of the skirting boards, doors and ceilings elevated each room. It worked well with the new natural off-white pastel colour on the walls contributing to the calm of the space. Long gone was the previous crazy red and coffee combination in the main bedroom and the purple and grey selection in the second bedroom. Little did I know that those colours tended to be some of the worst choices for a good night's sleep. Great for creativity and mental stimulation, apparently, but bottom of the list for relaxing and switching off. Ironically, the place was looking the best it had ever been – just as we handed it over to new owners to start their own journey. It's still strange to think that we lived there as it was, and yet made it better, nicer, for new owners. I couldn't help but think that it's living life in reverse somehow.

It didn't take long for an acceptable offer on the flat to be agreed once we put it on the market. One open day, two offers, a bit of negotiation and everything was concluded. The decision to sell the flat seemed so simple on reflection, however we did have to balance other people's opinions and weigh up how much effort it would be to keep hold of it and simultaneously rent it out. There were just too many variables to contend with to make it work: what if we couldn't get a tenant, what if they wanted to stay longer or shorter, what if we came home early, what if we came home later, what if repairs needed doing, what if they didn't pay the rent, how much would it all cost, etc, and, ultimately, the flat was the final thing keeping us tied to London, tied down, so, in the end, we decided to start our new life with a clean break. A new beginning was on the horizon and it felt easier to make that decision untethered, despite advice from friends and family to hold on to the "asset" and not jump off the property ladder. The whole point of our new path was to step off from traditional social ladders like this and jump on the bouncy castle of life instead. At any time, we could choose to step back on the ladder, if we wished, but our minds were made up: where we were going, we had no need for ladders.

I walked around each room slowly triple-checking everything of ours had gone, wiping clean any last bit of dust off windowsills and switching off plugs. I looked up into every corner to reassess the quality of my painting and cutting in. Average at best. I would probably give myself three stars out of five on the Checkatrade app. I checked the fridge and freezer to make sure there was no food left in the kitchen. I opened all the drawers and cupboards just for peace of mind that the place was completely empty and turned any remaining lights off. A decade of memories and experiences were in those rooms, my first home as a proper adult and the base for an education in life. So much had happened in this place, especially during its bachelor pad days – late-night parties, chilled-out Sundays; it's where I taught myself how to DJ and use editing software; play guitar and also complete *Guitar Hero* on expert level. The place hosted a lame Halloween scary movie party where a dozen or so people settled in to watch *The Human Centipede*. That was a weird evening. My old flatmate once stacked up all my stuff in front of my bedroom door one morning and as I opened it, piles of gear fell on top of me; maybe that was a sign then, if my mate could weaponise my stuff against me, maybe I had too much of it. I'd spent considerable time with a lot of people here in good times and bad and it was no surprise that I felt a little sentimental as I fiddled with the keys in my hand one final time. But that emotion was overshadowed by the exciting prospect of a new adventure. In an almost pivotal (and metaphorical) moment, I closed the front door behind me and, for the first time in a long time, I looked forward not backwards.

Dropping the keys off at the estate agent was a swift and pain-free task. Our agent walked us through the last few legalities and a timeline of the final steps. She shared her admiration of our plan and the other agents in the office all started chipping in with questions. They weren't used to seeing people this happy at letting go of something without replacing it with something else. Our search for that "something else" was just a little deeper than the average home buyer in the chain.

A final wish of good luck and an exchange of thank yous and we were done. The completion was finished, and we would shortly be heading back ten minutes up the road from our now old flat to my parents' house to stay there for a few days before flying out to Denmark and then on to Slovenia. I'd already signed off from work by then, had the standard leaving do in the pub that started early with a liquid lunch and finished late with blurred memories. I gave back my pass so it wouldn't remain lost in random pairs of trousers and also put on an out-of-office message that would hopefully brighten up someone's day.

Thanks for your email, I am currently out of the office for about a year. Right now, I could be on a beach in Panama City, I could be driving around Palm Springs, I may even be hiking through Vietnamese forests. You're more than welcome to hang around for a response but it's possible you may never get one. Alternatively, if you'd like to track me down and follow my adventure you can follow me on Instagram @ChristoLovett – it may be more interesting than the answer you're looking for. Once you've done following, feel free to contact Amanda, she'll probably be able to help, or at least forward you on to someone who can. Enjoy your day!

I'm sure they deactivated or suspended my email account shortly afterwards, but I did notice at least half a dozen new followers from work on the 'gram.

Some of the funds recouped from the sale of the flat would be the money we would use to start the next chapter. What started as just a conversation, a dream, was now close to turning into a reality. All it needed was an unconventional trade-off: Ditch a significant amount of physical stuff that had been cluttering up our living space, both of us step away from comfortable careers and then sell off the only home we've ever owned, without having another place to live permanently. Pretty much all the stability I'd ever known. In place of all the belongings and possessions we'd jettisoned would be new travel experiences and a whole bunch of future unknowns, and then progress in search of experiences without a long-term plan.

Simple.

As I walked out of the estate agents, Hayley held my hand. In the other, I looked down at my keyring and there was nothing there. No work fob, no pass, no house keys, no mailbox key, nothing.

I placed Souterrain on hold a few weeks before our first flight: no radio shows, no gigs and no development of artists. Not by me, at least. Jenna was more than happy to put our brand on ice for a bit as well so she could focus on renovating her new home and progressing her other real career. I could see she had started to lose motivation in it, so I sensed it was the beginning of the end for Souterrain, but we kept everything live just in case the break reinvigorated her passion for it. I had let the gig venue and boss at the radio station know so they could prepare alternatives. Although I was sharpening my ability to let go, I did briefly contemplate trying to make it work and run it all on my own whilst travelling. When I thought about managing all the communication and logistics, researching the artists, curating the gigs, negotiating fees, designing flyers and updating social media whilst travelling, I concluded that it was never going to be realistic. That idea of trying to have a good time sprinkled with always having to check email filled me full of anxiety and pressure, so putting the side hustle in a box for a while felt liberating and having one less thing to manage cleared space in my mind to absorb new things. To immerse myself into the adventure fully. No distractions.

The actual physical stuff that I owned had reduced dramatically. A suitcase of remaining clothes, a box of kitchen stuff and a handful of books were stashed at my mum and dad's house; other than that, we had very little. From a social status perspective, I had, willingly, let go of what society deemed as successful: owning a home, owning a car and having a job. Yes, I'd left the door open to go back to work when I returned – I was only on sabbatical, after all – but by making this step, I had pretty much signalled that my future lay elsewhere. But what that future was, I had no idea. I knew there would be a new job on my return, so you could say it was a round trip geographically, but a one-way ticket mentally. Hayley's perspective was very black and white; she had hit pause on her whole career by purposefully walking away from her media job. She was officially unemployed. How exciting. How fucking terrifying.

For the first time in my adult life, I was debt free. In the past, every time I got close to paying off my credit cards (notice plural), something expensive would get in the way, like Christmas, for example. Or a holiday. Or the MOT on the car. Every year it peeked its head around the corner and every year I'd say, "I'm not going to go mad this Christmas," before spending hundreds of pounds on theatre tickets and, while I was there, I'd treat myself to a little something, you know, "just because". I always felt like I was in control, knowing that if I wanted to, I could clear those credit card debts within a few months. Much like a gambler or smoker, I had convinced myself that I could stop at any time, however, the purchase of the possession was too important and so the debt would just tick over each month. I'd subsequently spent years and lots of money bringing it back down. Having never defaulted on any payments and always trying to clear more than the minimum, paying sums off the credit card was just added to the rest of the outgoings, so it became an unavoidable monthly bill, like a utility or council tax. It even got added to the bills spreadsheet Hayley and I once set up, and then promptly ignored. In a weird way, I also thought that I was winning at something. The credit card game is set up to praise you for being a good citizen and playing your part in borrowing. For years, I was awarded the highest possible credit score with Experian, 999. Ironic, isn't it, that it's also the same number you would ring in an emergency. We, as consumers, get rewarded for borrowing by being offered the opportunity to take out a loan.

"Well done for paying off your debts…fancy a bit more?"

Right then, and for the immediate future, there were no more minimum payments, no more high-interest mortgage outgoings, no more setting half my salary aside for purchasing mistakes made in the past. It could have been short lived but all that went away, and I embraced the freedom that being debt free gave me.

I'd hit the reset button on life. I had purged many of my possessions. It should have all felt scary and intimidating. But, instead, it felt exhilarating.

9. Packing Habits

Hayley and I had managed to borrow some large backpacks from a couple of friends who had been travelling before but, luckily for us, who had no immediate plans on using them. Our packing strategy was to take two large bags to hold all our clothes and shoes, plus a small backpack each for electricals, books, water bottles, chargers, snacks and general wandering around. Although I had ditched some clothing over the previous few months, my options were still pretty vast. Having never been away from home for longer than a couple of weeks, I had no idea how much stuff I needed to take for a ten-month travelling adventure, so my default was to take everything. Every eventuality needed to be covered, I thought, plus a bit more just in case plus a disaster kit for the unknown. Over the previous remaining weeks, I had read several articles and watched a few YouTube videos about packing for travelling. The consistent theme was to take less than what you would initially think. Of course, I thought I knew better so I started to cram a bunch of clothing into the larger of the two bags which had been designated for me. Whilst I had been able to donate a large portion of clothes from my collection, I did it in the mindset of knowing my immediate future. I did it knowing that I'd be fine without them because I was totally in control of my surroundings, the places I went to and the people I saw. It was easier to be rational when I was in a place of certainty: my home. Packing for the unknown almost made me regress a little and I wanted to ease the discomfort of the impending new places and cultures by overcompensating with extra home comforts. Maybe if I took more of my clothes, I'd retain more of my identity, I thought. Maybe it was the whole "safety in numbers" thing, but with clothes?

I laid the bag on the floor of my parent's spare bedroom and unzipped the zips as far back as they went. Their sturdiness was not lost on me. My carrying companion was my new best friend, a blank canvas of volcanic grey only interrupted by its white logo, a simply drawn bird of prey with wings outstretched. The bird represented a sense of freedom with the ability to be found on all continents. That connection was also not lost on me. I pushed out the inner layers and removed any internal buckles so I could take stock of how much space I had to play with. Looking around the room at all the things I wanted to take, I was slightly deluded that they would all fit in this bag, but I was willing to give it a go anyway.

The first layer was already set, an excessive number of toiletries and a bulging first-aid kit. Then went the footwear, a white pair of high-top Converse, flip-flops, a pair of running trainers and a pair of brown shoes. I also packed a pair of black Nikes, so five in total. Stuffed into each shoe were two or three pairs of socks, ranging from white ankle trainer socks to black smart dress socks. In all, we were looking at twenty pairs. I built protection around the footwear by folding up every single piece of underwear I owned, sliding it into any gaps in the bag where I could fit my hand. Shorts, jeans and chinos went next. Four pairs of different-coloured shorts, my swimming shorts, tan chinos and four pairs of jeans, grey, black and two blue, got added. I would wear skinny tracksuit bottoms on the plane. Twenty-five t-shirts were delicately placed on top; my favourite ones I packed carefully between others so as not to ruin them. At that stage the height of the contents already topped the height of the bag. No matter what the 'experts' had said in the blogs and on the videos, I still believed they were wrong, and I was right, so I carried on packing as much as I could.

Some jumpers were laid on top and then covered by a rain mac which had its own bag. I placed one small coat over it and then started to fold up some shirts. I decided to take a mixture of smart and casual shirts, eight in total. They were laid on top just because I had a habit of always packing shirts last. Finally, I decided to take two hats that I'd not worn in years, one a brown pork pie with a black ribbon and the other a charcoal trilby with a feather and small fake carnation on the side. Fancy.

"Why are you taking those?" Hayley laughed, quite rightly, as she sat next to her full but zipped-up bag. She had chosen the smaller of the two backpacks and finished packing a while ago. She had been observing me fold, pack, move, unpack, rinse and repeat for at least the last twenty minutes. I felt her eyes judging me.

I didn't have a good enough answer.

I huffed and puffed and snorted loudly.

Her challenge led me to start all over again. I slowly started to take out most of the clothing I had just carefully placed in so I could make room for the hats.

An hour went by and I was no closer to figuring out the optimal packing arrangement that didn't cause serious creasing to the headwear, the shoes or the shirts. Every time I felt that I was close to completing the task, either the zips didn't close properly, or the bag weighed too much. Those poor zips had been pulled and pushed relentlessly; I was surprised they didn't buckle under the stress of it all. Hayley had been in and out of the room, had lunch, made a few calls, while I was no closer to finishing at all.

I was at a crossroads again. Sat on the floor surrounded by piles of stuff, clothes this time, re-folding items up that I hadn't worn in years, but I wondered whether the trip could be where that unloved t-shirt or unused pair of shorts would be relaunched back into the world. The same scenario was projected for the hats as they rested nicely on top of a pile of underwear.

The larger items were clearly the shoes and the bulky jeans but at each attempt, I filtered out a pair of socks or a t-shirt that I could just about live without. I was avoiding making the big decisions by covering them up with lots of little ones. It was false progress. On the face of it, it looked as though I was taking less but it made very little difference to the end result. The zips could still not complete their journey around the bag. I contemplated putting the hats in my smaller backpack but that would mean I'd have to remove other things like the iPad and chargers that were already settled. I thought that maybe wearing one would solve the dilemma but then I'd have to take it off regularly. A trilby hat and tracksuit combination sounded quite daring but not one I, or the world, was totally ready for yet.

I also didn't want to be held up at airport security with some hairy guard pulling me to one side asking, "Excuse me, fella, why are you wearing two hats?"

"Here's an idea, maybe don't take the hats?" Hayley said, now half frustrated, half in fits of laughter at my indecision. She knew this would bamboozle me.

There was a simple solution to this predicament that I had caused for myself, but it wasn't that easy to concede. If the hats didn't play a role in the biggest experience of my life, it meant that they were likely never that important anyway. It was quite the realisation. I had built these hats up so much that their status had risen from just being an accessory to an extension of my mind, body and soul.

After one final over-extravagant exhale of annoyance, eventually I agreed to leave the hats behind and with the shuffling around of a few more things I managed to just close the backpack.

I shifted responsibility onto Hayley and told her that if there's a night out while we're away where one of the hats would have been perfect, she's to blame. I was being serious.

She laughs and shrugs. "Whatever."

There was a small sense of loss, even though the hats would still be here when I returned. I hadn't discarded them; I'd just chosen not to use them this time.

I guess back then, I joined the other 65 percent of people who found this part of the trip to be the most stressful, according to a study conducted by OnePoll. The study also mentioned that over-packing was another area that seems to be an issue for travellers, with around a quarter of stuff taken remaining unused or untouched.

At the time, the two hats were nothing but a trivial moment, quickly forgotten about, but now they represent just another incident of choosing less in exchange for progress. I do remember being able to take myself out of the situation and project forwards in time, seeing myself still having an amazing adventure without the hats being there. I removed the hats from the make-believe future and in doing so, found it easier to let go. Once I saw a picture, it made me believe that everything was going to be fine without them. The truth was I hadn't worn them for a really long time and in the end, two inanimate objects almost caused an issue. You could say they nearly took ownership of me, but in the end, I took back control and left them behind, with intention. Fuck you, hats.

I wrestled the closed bag onto my shoulders to test its weight (and my resilience) and toppled back just a little. I recalibrated myself and stood up straight, proud that I could withstand the pull of my possessions. As a test, I walked up and down the stairs just to prove to myself that I could manage the force and not cause myself an injury. It was also a show of defiance to prove to others that I was right to be taking the volume I was taking.

What I carried on my back was a whole load of indecision, a need for acceptance and stress. The physical items in the bag were a manifestation of my mental clutter and years of collecting clothing to enforce my safe place in society. The path ahead was not as well-lit as it once was, but I was striding forward, bravely taking more risks. As I did that, I was being held back a little by the comfort zone I was carrying, low risk and low reward. Even though I had less, there was still some weight behind me, holding me back from truly being able to detach from the value I placed on my material possessions and identity. I was letting go one small step at a time. What I needed was a giant leap...

August 16, 2017. The day of our first flight had arrived. It was a quieter morning than I would have thought, I remember, as my nervousness led me to take longer than expected to print my own boarding pass at the machine. I was reading the clear instructions on how to place my passport onto the scanner with more intensity than I would read anything else. My dad started to help Hayley with her luggage tag whilst my mum asked, for the fifteenth time, "Are you sure you've got everything?"

I noticed she said, 'everything'.

With the boarding pass printed we were finally good to go. We placed our backpacks on ready for the short walk to the bag-drop desk in the north terminal of Gatwick airport. My mum and dad had kindly driven us to see us off. As we unloaded the excess of our backs and lowered them on the scales, we nervously smiled at the member of staff as they weighed our bags. It would be the first of many check-ins, the first of a few nervous moments as we would watch the numbers flicker up and down calculating the weight – the burden of the lives we were carrying with us.

We passed with flying colours, just. The scales tipping point rested in our favour.

Copenhagen awaited.

Despite passing level one, I was still constantly checking things about my person were in order. I took my passport out of my denim jacket pocket and then put it back in another pocket. Moments later I would pad down my chest for reassurance that it was still there, and I'd forgotten I'd moved it somewhere else. That split-second of panic was so strange; I knew I had it on me, but the excessive checking was bordering on OCD. My anxiety levels were elevated, and I was not sure if it was just an airport thing or whether it was the magnitude of the journey. Between Hayley and me we had a lot of information, either printed off or accessible on our phones. Hotel bookings, car rentals, train journeys, visas, everything you could think of was stored some-where safe. We knew everything was present and correct but that feeling of needing to check things repeatedly, to feel that feeling of reassurance, would only subside when we landed in Denmark. I was longing to throw off the shackles of reassurance and feel unburdened by the anxiety. I wanted to feel that sense of carefree nonchalance that came with adventuring – *que sera sera* – "whatever will be will be".

I looked over to check where we needed to go next and my parents began to tear up.

The only time I'd seen my dad cry was when Chelsea won the Premier League in 2005. A fifty-year wait from the last time they'd been champions. Whether it was my mum starting him off or not I didn't know but he pulled me in and squeezed out a big hug. This trip was a big thing for Hayley and me, but it was only then that I realised the impact it would have on my parents. It would be a significant journey for them too. This was just one massive change in a line of recent changes they had watched me complete: selling the flat, pretty much walking away from a 'successful' career and ditching the majority of everything I owned. Part of them must have thought I had gone mad. They questioned a lot of my actions as it was all foreign to them. This wasn't how you did life in their book.

I'd never been more than a forty-five-minute drive away from them, and now I was leaving everything behind. I'm also certain my parents believed that we might not return. That something would happen while I was away – good or bad – which meant I would never see them again, or I would decide to live in Myanmar or Canada or Laos forever. In that moment, I should have tried to explain that I would always be within the metaphorical arms' reach, but I didn't. I was too absorbed in my excitement to reduce their fears. For them, the unknown always filled them with tension. Going west was OK, they had been to Canada and the USA before so their experience of it was personal, they felt safe there so projected that safety onto us. Asia, on the other hand, was a mystery to them so all they had to go on was stories from the news. There was the ongoing conflict in the north of Myanmar, where we were going later on in the trip, but thankfully nowhere near those troubles, but they would have still worried. As we swiftly checked our backpacks again, we waved goodbye to them one last time and moved our way through the security and headed to the place most travellers go before a flight: the departure lounge pub.

Beer tastes different at an airport. I'm sure the quality is the same, but it's generally mixed with morning toothpaste, anticipation and excitement, and that combo made that particular lager taste a little sweeter. An airport is one of the few places that drinking at 7am is acceptable, encouraged even. You know you'll regret it when you need a piss ten minutes into the flight but what else can you do to kill the time? There's only so much perusing of sunglasses, bags and duty free you can do.

To kill even more time, I logged in and checked my online bank balance.

I'd become obsessed with checking my bank balance over the previous few months. At least once a day I'd check each app to see if there was any movement, making sure there was enough to cater for the variety of outgoings that travel planning brought. I'd also started to buy fewer material things, so I was more intentional where I was spending my money. Whilst Hayley was on the phone to her mum, and in between sips of cold morning lager, I checked our travel spreadsheet again, proud of what we had achieved to make this all happen. The very last tab of the spreadsheet was labelled "Bonus Money", a little section I kept open to track any incomings that were outside of general wages that we grafted to help finance this trip.

I slowly absorbed the entries and started to add it up. The total amount brought in just from the sale of unused items in our home generated £685. Using a cashback site when purchasing flights, hotels, rental cars, insurance and other unavoidable outgoings generated an additional £400. One that I was particularly proud of was getting £565 through compensation after a series of complaints to companies who ballsed up. The extra cash raised would go a long way in some of the countries in Asia we were headed to and it was all sourced from a slight change of attitude and a good shot of courage.

I had become sick and tired of just accepting things. Playing the victim, you could say. No longer would I just drift along, passively being a part-time player in my own life and hope that everything would work out for me and the people close to me. For the first time ever, I was starting to stand up for myself. If anyone gave me shit service, or I felt that I, or others, were wronged in any way, I would call people out on it. When our internet provider took a payment after we had asked our account to be cancelled, I was on it. Delays in orders or minor errors on purchases, whatever it was, I didn't let a thing go. I now had a glimpse of this assertiveness, resilience and sense of self-worth that was hidden away, probably underneath all of my crap. It was like I was Jim Carrey in *The Truman Show* feeling trapped in familiarity and constantly battling with a continuously compliant identity. Truman (spoiler alert) ended up finding sufficient awareness to leave home and in doing so developed a more authentic identity, and I had started to feel the same. Sitting there, on the edge of the unknown, was an understanding that having more belief in myself and knowing I was of value quickly made me realise that this new behaviour shift gave immediate rewards, not just financially but mentally. I felt heard, I felt a little braver and more confident each time I challenged something from a place of curiosity and positivity. My intention was never to slam anyone or any company, I get that mistakes happen, but it became my responsibility to hold up the mirror. My words became more deliberate and I quickly found a system that helped me break down the issue, explain calmly how it had negatively impacted me or others and politely demand to be compensated for helping them to rectify the problem for me, and subsequently for others in the future. Still to this day, I use this life skill to remain strong and authentic in moments of conflict. Just last week, I had to rectify an issue with my bank, a mistake which caused stress and concern, so I politely asked them to fix it and compensate me for the time and effort it took to highlight it to them.

Debt free and an additional £1,650 in just eight months from the start of 2017, just through being a bit more intentional with money, decluttering all the unused and unloved stuff as well as showing some integrity to my values a bit more. Not bad, I thought.

Hayley passed the phone over to me and I chatted with her mum for a couple of minutes. She wished us a safe journey and expressed how she couldn't wait to hear how it all pans out. After the usual five or six "Byes'" later I hung up the phone.

"What are you smiling at?" Hayley asked as I picked up my lager and put down the phone.

"I think we've done fucking brilliant to make this happen, I'm so proud of us," I said, full of glee. And Estrella.

"It's mad, isn't it? We had all that stuff sitting there the whole time," Hayley responded, sipping on a rather large glass of white wine. Apparently, to "help her sleep on the plane".

A few moments later our gate number flashed up on the screen. We finished our drinks and collected our things together. Of course, our gate was the furthest away so after a leisurely ten-minute trek, interrupted only by a brief pointless foot race between us to get to the end of one of the moving walkways, we arrived at our little enclosed space to see people already boarding the plane. We casually joined the back of the queue with passports and boarding passes in hand.

"You ready?" Hayley asked with a smile and raised eyebrows.

"FUCK! I've lost my passpo… na, I'm ready." I responded, casually, anticipating a dig on the arm or a loving insult in response.

"You dickhead."

There it was.

"Let's do it."

PHASE THREE

Revelation

"You sell off the kingdom piece by piece and trade it for a horse that will take you anywhere."
Colin Wright, Author and Podcast Host

10. The Wishing Tree

The squeak of my Converse became more prominent as we felt the burn of a 250-foot incline from San Francisco's Mission District on the way to the Castro, a prominent LGBTQ borough. Each time I planted my right foot, my Converse squeaked. I tried to make a slight adjustment to the angle of how it landed on the pavement in an attempt to stifle the annoying sound. The root of the noise was from a combination of my sock and the heel on the inside of my high top and I didn't know if I had only just noticed it or whether the material had only just worn away. Whatever it was, it was as unwanted as a loud chewer.

We swung a right from twenty-fourth street onto Castro and headed up through Noe Valley. Taking in the comfortable and partly sunny twenty-two degrees, Hayley and I strolled slowly up the wide sidewalk admiring the local community essence, the smells, the buildings and locals. Every block was on an incline but as you reached the crosswalks they flattened out. A number of different-coloured staircases at slight angles led up into levelled-off front porches of Victorian houses which displayed light blues, maroon, light greens, whites and shades of grey. The average price for a house in this area was in excess of $2million. It's night and day when compared to a couple of miles down the road where we were staying. The Tenderloin district was the wild fucking west. Bordering some of the wealthiest neighbourhoods, this forgotten part of the city was like an episode of *The Wire*. Open drug-dealing on street corners, controlled by gangs, was taking place outside our hostel window. We'd gotten accustomed to the different drugs that dealers were selling. One dealer attracted the attention of potential buyers with a high-pitched whistle. Further down the street another dealer chose a deep holler in an attempt to draw attention to his offerings of meth, fentanyl and heroin.

The fire service were generally the first responders to an old run-down hotel across the street. They supported the paramedics with first aid on lifeless overdosed bodies that they calmly transferred from the building into the back of whatever vehicle was closest. The composed manner of the skilled emergency services indicated to us that these scenarios were not a rare occurrence.

Dozens of used syringes scattered the sidewalks as passers-by navigated the out-of-control homeless problem, human shit and overflowing trash to get to their intended destination. This was rock bottom for those who resided here, preyed upon by dealers and discarded by the authorities. It appeared that the folk who hung around here were moved away from the touristic Union Square, pushed down a few blocks so as to not be seen by holiday makers who wanted to flash their cash. The pace of walking quickened around here, and we kept our eyes firmly on the end of the street when heading out. By day it was an open-air narcotics market, by night the tortured souls came out and were doubled over on the sidewalk in what I can only describe as a refugee camp. In front of them was an assortment of bric-a-brac laid out, which I assumed was for sale. This was fifteen minutes away from billionaires' row – Twitter and Uber HQ. It was an incredibly sad situation and a glimpse of what you get when you look behind the curtain.

"When you walk out of here, go right, do not go left," the hostel receptionist warned us.

It would be a scene that made me ponder about how I could help others with whatever skills I had to offer. In that setting, I didn't know how I could help. I didn't have any expertise or knowledge of homelessness, drugs or mental health issues. I only thought about me, and mine and Hayley's safety. I had no idea whether there was anything I could do, but looking back now, donating some of my unwanted gear hopefully helped charities and experts who were in a better place directly back home to support, and so relinquishing my desire for stuff would have added value to local communities. And it still does today. Hopefully, writing this book and sharing my story of less inspires others to donate their unwanted things to charities and through the coaching I now do with various people, that also unlocks their ability to be more and achieve more with less. Now I know that decluttering and being more conscious about purchases is not just good for us as individuals and families, it's good for communities and the environment as well.

· · · · · ⓢ · · · · ·

Cars climbed their way up through each well-manicured block and paused at crossings before straining to pull away up the next hill. Every now and then we heard a scrape of a front grille grinding on the cement as cars made their way down the peaks. We didn't see many others walking up these streets, there were no famous landmarks or big hotels attracting visitors to this part of town. The steep hills between Castro and the Mission districts prompted people to take other forms of travel. As the strolling went from relaxing to a workout, I began to understand why they'd take the tram or jump in their cars.

Red and green sweetshade trees had been planted symmetrically on each side of the road; they were in full bloom and their leafiness stretched over parked cars and wide sidewalks. They'd been placed with precision urban design in mind, no sign of roots or any pavement cracks. Hints of orange and jasmine aromas struck me through the air as I strolled past. We let a couple of cars go before we strode confidently across the crosswalk, knowing which way to look to safely make our way. Each block looked similar but as I crossed twenty-third street more bright colours appeared in my periphery and grabbed my attention.

"Hold up a sec," I said to Hayley. "There's something down this street."

We took a right and started to walk down another tree-lined village in the city. More beautiful four- and five-bedroom houses stretched up and out. The sidewalks were pristine, and the trees again cut the concrete with their shade. One in the distance caught my eye. This one tree was different, it didn't hang the same way as the others; from this distance it looked like there was something in or on it. My pace quickened and I saw hundreds of pieces of pink, blue, yellow and white paper hanging from the branches. I wondered if there was a celebration of some sort and a local resident had decided to decorate this tree. Only this tree. Closer and closer with each step the colours became more vivid and more detail of the contents of the tree revealed itself. The bits of paper had writing on. I took one in my hand.

"I wish for a healthy life for my friends and family."

I picked up another. "I wish my dearest friend finds peace."

Above that another white tag displayed, "I wish that Erik and I will last forever."

Down this quiet street away from the hustle and bustle of San Francisco life was the Noe Valley Wishing Tree. Standing alone, independent, strong and elegant.

Hayley and I spent the next ten minutes reading out the written wishes.

"I wish I'll finish school and marry the love of my life."

"I wish for confidence!"

"I wish for inner peace for me and my wife."

"Freedom for dreamers."

"I wish for love and no wars."

"I wish I was Beyoncé!"

At the base of the tree was a small black chalkboard that read, "Make a wish…" in white lettering with a heart in the corner. Next to the sign was an empty glass jar. I picked up the jar and showed Hayley whilst at the same time pulling a sad clown face. There were no more markers to be seen and all the tags had been used up.

"I wish there was more stationery," I said to Hayley with a fake laugh, putting my pinkie finger to the corner of my mouth á la Dr. Evil.

The tree looked as if it had around 500 tags on it already, each one with its own individual wish. Some were humorous, a few ineligible, but most were poignant and humble. A lot of people had spent some time here thinking about their personal contribution to the world. The tags on the side of the tree facing the road had started to fade in the sun.

This tree was an idea by a three-year-old who lived in the house opposite. Apparently, the infant kept making lots of wishes indoors so her mum told her to put some of them on the tree outside their home.

The first wish on the tree from the child was apparently asking for a giraffe. Why not aim high, right? Pretty soon after, the family put out a jar with tags, ribbons and markers and prompted neighbours to write their own wishes. By the end of day one, twelve wishes were attached.

It looked like most people in and around the neighbourhood had taken part and maybe taken a souvenir pen as well. The tree appeared to have become a beacon of hope, a place for aspirations, a place for intention, for inspiration and second chances. It was a place where people could tell their story and share their feelings without judgement. This tree also symbolised a place to stop and think. Distracted by the constant pressure of living busy lives, it was nice to create that space to pause. Just for a moment. And reflect. Ponder. Contemplate. Breathe. I was disappointed that we were not able to leave our mark on this neighbourhood in the hope of inspiring anyone who read our tag, but equally as happy to have experienced it. Sometimes, going slightly off track can add some positive surprises.

As we walked back towards the main road, I thought carefully about what wish I would have written, pondering my over-thinking, my remaining self-doubt and the constant desire to be doing things.

I wish I could stop thinking about work, I thought, what I may or may not be missing out on or what job to do next. I wish I could just stop the negative self-talk, I wish I could stop worrying about what's going to happen with Souterrain, I wish I could just stop thinking about where on earth we live next. I wish I could just stop the mental clutter and the over-thinking.

I wish I could just... stop.

11. Slow Travel

This tour was starting to become different. What may have, at first, initially felt like an extended holiday, had now evolved into something more sensory. I'd allowed myself to become absorbed by the different cultural sounds of traffic, languages and music. My palette had already expanded to experience new food combinations I'd never encountered before, such as poutine, a traditional dish from Quebec consisting of French fries, cheese curds and gravy. One portion of that was plenty for dinner! I felt more of a sense of community, reconnecting and spending time with extended family in Nova Scotia as well as hanging out with the locals at The Presidio in San Francisco. The touch of grass, pavement, bottles, it was just all different and it really was an education for my senses. I could feel myself becoming more carefree, less connected to the old me.

The days had one or two key things on our To-Do, must-see, must-visit list but other than that, the choice of activities remained up to how we felt on that day. It was a different approach from previous holidays or breaks where we crammed as many tourist spots into our week away as possible to feel that sense of accomplishment. On this trip, it didn't matter what we accomplished – the journey was more important than the destination. Living in the moment was more precious than filling the moment with things to do. I remember previous trips to places like Rome, and reporting to friends that we had "done" Rome or "ticked off" the popular areas in Barcelona. As if they themselves were To-Do lists – items to complete, rather than enjoy. On those trips I'd been even more knackered coming home than before I left. I had just transitioned the franticness of my life at home to another location. And, of course, I would overpack and take my clutter with me. Now I had learnt to slow down and enjoy each minute in the moment.

This slower approach to travel had just started to become apparent organically when we arrived in Yosemite. We were engulfed by the sheer magnitude of nature wrapping itself around us. Our compact vehicle was laughable compared to the bulk and muscle of other SUVs and trucks in our rear view but the Toyota Yaris we hired was comfortable and economical. Plus, it was cheaper to hire than most of the other fancy cars on offer. The Yaris was a mini-beast on the mean San Francisco streets. With its help, I mastered the art of driving on the wrong (right) side of the road. Turning right on a red light was also a new skill to add to the driving repertoire. Other than an awkward twenty minutes figuring out how to pump gas in Groveland, driving had been a surprisingly enjoyable addition to the trip. Getting behind the wheel and cruising down huge stretches of road and meandering through mountains was something I'd never done before. For me, driving was just something that I did to get from one place to another, a means to an end. The unavoidable. Getting to the destination was the goal and once there, that's where the party started. On this trip, I learnt that exploring was just as important as completing the objective.

As we snaked through vast rock formations and the humbling Sierra Nevada peaks, we picked up local radio stations and, wanting to immerse ourselves fully into our surroundings, we ended up listening to hours of country music. It became our travel soundtrack.

I still have a Spotify playlist featuring the sounds of 'Fix A Drink' by Chris Janson, 'I'll Name the Dogs' by Blake Shelton, 'Wagon Wheel' by Darius Rucker and 'When It Rains It Pours' by Luke Combs as well as another two hours of country hits from the summer of 2017.

We were in awe of the scenery and often pulled over to the side of the road to stop and take it in. Even this small behaviour was new, and it took a few times to remove the twitch to just jump out, take a picture and get back in the car.

Slow it down. Breathe it in, I thought. Let the eyes absorb every colour and surface.

The fact that we didn't have to be anywhere at any particular time helped.

There were no dinner plans with friends, no places to be by a certain time, it was just us. And we got to choose what we did. I began to enjoy my more leisurely mindset. We purposely took the longer, scenic routes to places so we could enjoy the drive. Within our self-designed structure of time and budget, we had become creators. Having laid out the rough bookends – the flights either end – what filled the shelf was determined by us and how we felt. In that moment. If we wanted to get up at 5am and watch colourful hot-air balloons fill the skies, we did. If we wanted to stay in bed and wake up at lunch time, that was our decision to make. We accepted the fact that we were not going to see and do everything. And we didn't want to. That realisation of not feeling as though we missed out on anything made us more in tune with what we did do, and it was a feeling that filled my body with quiet satisfaction.

Just being behind the wheel on an open road with no particular place to go felt different than it ever had before. Often, on holiday, it would take a few days to really wind down from day-to-day life – that moment where it turned into a holiday – and then as we were on the back end, we clicked back into the previous default mode again. Behind the wheel though, I began to truly feel I was no longer watching life go by, I was living each moment out loud.

I felt connected to the road. More connected to the journey than the destination. A classic cliché but it rang true for me. I'd become more open to exploring new connections with the culture, local food and people within the communities. Only a few months prior, my life would have been considered fast. Although my exterior, my personality, would portray a sense of calm and consideration, inside it was everything you would associate with pace, impatience, hurry and stress. I now call it my "fast food" period. Everything was about speed, not taste. I would tell everyone I was calm, but I would rarely feel it. This adjustment in my mindset, brought on by the freedom of travel, felt a lot better and there was less desire to rush around and risk burnout. I felt more motivated to experience a place more deeply rather than get in, tick off the landmark and leave. Being more intentional about this mindset and way of travel allowed me to collect new things, gave me a moment to pause, be flexible and make the journey – dare I say it – meaningful. Everything I did was no longer reactive – it was intentional, pre-emptive.

· · · · · ⓢ · · · · · ·

There had not been one cloud in the early October sky all day and we'd clocked up another twenty-odd kilometres strolling through the pine forests and orangey-red sandstone this area was famous for. Hayley was asleep in the passenger seat after another long hike through the red rock secret mountain wilderness at Coconino National Park, Sedona.

George, the massage therapist, yogi-shaman and mystic healer we were staying with for a few days, recommended we take a certain path on the hike and his suggestion was bang on. We'd been warmly welcomed into his home (or "healing retreat", as he called it), which was covered with spiritual and meditation decor. Dreamcatchers hung from every door and wind chimes and hammocks swayed in the breeze on the front porch. Bongos and guitars hung on the wall in the living room alongside huge tapestries of varying colours. Singing crystal bowls and one large Tibetan bowl were sprinkled around various rooms. A didgeridoo was leant up against the sofa to complete his unique feng shui. George saw my interest in the instrument when we arrived and invited me to try it out. Of course, having never played a didgeridoo before I was woeful at it, but I blamed my now-long beard for the interference in the airways. George took the wind instrument away from me and gave us a blast; he was clearly an expert. By doing so, he established himself as the alpha male in front of Hayley, his mate Trent and another guest named Donna who was staying in a bedroom down the hall. I discovered that she was a "digital nomad" who made her own jewellery whilst travelling around the country. I liked that term and wondered – once I knew what it was – if I could ever be a digital nomad, someone who worked from their laptop as they travelled? Positive energy and vibrations were the essence of this place and although my previous risk-averse mindset in the past would have been somewhat sceptical and uncomfortable in retreats like this, it was now welcomed and by luck or judgement we were connecting with the unique culture of the area and its highly creative people.

We had to trade in the Yaris as the rear bumper started to fall off on the I-10 from Palm Springs. Maybe Hayley and I both got a little too overconfident with the huge stretches of highway and started to speed our way through the state alongside trucks, lorries and other beefy American vehicles. Our poor little Yaris was good to us. Through some more convincing, the rental firm switched us over to whatever they had available at no extra cost (looking back this was another example of standing up for myself and not accepting an inferior position), so our replacement was a fresh 2.4-litre Kia Optima, a saloon, and a considerable upgrade from the dinky Yaris. With more room throughout, the Optima made it easier for the passenger to take a quick nap during long stints of highway or after a tiring hike.

They say that the energy in Sedona is different, special, maybe. Apparently, it has meditative and inspirational qualities. The legend of the four metaphysical vortexes are thought to be swirling centres of energy that can leave you feeling rejuvenated. Whether that's a crock of shit or not, I didn't know, but being outside in this serene location certainly did make me feel appreciative of where I was. The digital clock in the Optima read 4.31pm and we were stuck in a less than energetic traffic jam listening to a local radio station that played 90s R 'n' B. I didn't know the particular tune that was playing but I could tell by the distinctive drum-machine rhythms that it was from that golden era and, if I had to choose, my favourite genre. In the stillness of the one-way gridlock, I opened my window and inhaled the ambience.

With absolutely no cars coming the other way, it allowed me a great view of the desert town's psychedelic, multi-coloured steep canyon walls. The base, a blaze of fiery red, softened as it reached the peak and distinctive contours split the varying shades like a carefully crafted palette. The formations reached into a sea of blue skies erupting out of the dense green pine beneath. Unspoilt.

This view was one of the best things I had ever seen.

I stared longingly at it for what seemed an eternity. So as not to disturb Hayley's sleep, I turned the radio down to a mere background muffle and in that moment, it was like I'd turned down all the inner noise as well. My chest expanded as I took a slower, deeper breath. As I slowed the car down, to less than a crawl, the breeze of the desert air manoeuvred itself around my sun-kissed arm causing the hairs to stand on end. In deep grid-lock, I brought the car to a halt with no idea how long the delay would be. I slowly opened and closed my left hand, stretching out my palm as the warm and calming air danced through my outstretched fingers, testing the strength of the fabrics on my bracelet. That moment was the most content I had felt in a long time. Perhaps ever. Everything was right where it needed to be. I felt lighter in myself, my appreciation of the surroundings was heightened. I felt more in tune. It was not just a change in feeling because of all the vortexes but this had been building over the last couple of weeks, months.

This was it.

I had come to a complete standstill, literally and metaphorically. I was in the moment.

A traffic jam in the Arizona desert had just given me the final nudge to stay right where I was and to enjoy the now-ness of it all. The smells of the road, the environment, the touch on the steering wheel, the view, the everyday things I took for granted had now become acknowledged, admired and enjoyed. The awareness of myself and the surroundings in this moment were levelled up and a new state of discovery presented itself.

In that moment, my mind was empty of all previous chaos

and I couldn't have been more content. There was no mental clutter, no noise, the limitations pertained to my self-doubt and fear had gone. The blocks had gone, and I didn't care where. Everywhere I had gone before, I was still there, my internal limitations followed me around. But now, that outward journey of freedom and slow travel combined with this new internal realisation of freedom in this almost meditative state, had made me acknowledge those inner thoughts for what they were. False noise. I was not thinking about the past, I was not thinking about the future, I was just present.

I think of this moment every day. Whenever I need to feel focus, I return to that moment of stillness and relive it.

For others, their 'happy place' may be a beach, a gorgeous sunset or a park bench – mine was in fucking traffic. Is yours as ridiculous as this?

A gentle beep from the car behind me pulled my attention into reality again as I looked ahead on the road to notice a significant gap where the vehicles in front had already moved on. Whatever had caused the delay now seemed to have been removed. The distance between me and the car in front started to open up, which prompted me to put the car back into drive and I carefully stepped on the gas and woke the vehicle out of its own slumber. Creeping forwards I took another longing look out the window, as the moment and personal painting of the rocks melted back into the background. I switched my focus back onto the road, turning the radio volume up a little to wake up the mind. Even though it was just sitting in a car waiting in traffic, in that meditative moment my mind was free and undistracted. Untethered from the chaos of life.

Free from noises of fear, judgement, time, plans and expectations. In that brief moment, I had finally unlocked the combined body and mind feeling of real freedom. Whenever I see, or sit, in traffic now, I never see it as a complication, or frustration, I see it for what it really is: a moment to sit still and embrace the fact that, in that moment, there is nowhere else you can be.

Have you slowed down yet?

12. Slovenian Parcel

The Slovenian city of Kranj was a short ride from Ljubljana air-port. The darkness of the winter night was only interrupted by a light snow shower which had carpeted the ground in an off-white. Footprints on the pavement and tyre tracks on the roads helped the snow turn into slush as we carefully traversed our way across the small bridge into the centre of the fourth largest city in the country. A few lights were on as we strolled around quiet buildings but because it was zero-degrees Celsius, the streets were desolate. Christmas lights swayed in the harsh wind between buildings as the city prepared for its end-of-year festivities, but they were yet to be turned on. Alleyways protected us from the cold blast as we dodged puddles of melted ice, looking for our resting place for the next thirty-six hours. Carrying our heavy backpacks in the freezing cold night trying not to slip over was not my idea of a fun evening. We were now five months into our journey and we finally arrived at the place where we weren't supposed to be. I was deep into the reality of that mentally cluttered Sunday morning flight-booking mistake just under a year ago whilst lying in bed. Although we rectified the timings and changed our initial direc-tion of travel, the only reason we were back in Slovenia again was to fly to Myanmar. It was a stark contrast to the summer when we were less than twenty miles away in the beautiful Lake Bled, the second stop on our tour, attending our friends' wedding before leaving all our mates behind and flying to Toronto, kicking off the next part of our own adventure. It also felt a million miles away from the daily shorts and t-shirt weather we had enjoyed then, as well as a mere forty-eight hours ago in Atlanta, Georgia. Because this part of the journey was a mistake, our brief stay didn't give us too long to explore the area and it wasn't going to be long before we connected with our flights and started the second part of the odyssey. And, yes, by this point, our adventure had grown from a trip to a full-blown voyage of self-discovery.

We were tired and weary travellers with bags still so full they were a constant source of pain. Packing, arriving at destination, unpacking, was the rinse-repeat cycle we had grown accustomed to. Each time we found it more difficult than the last and every time, without fail, I felt a shoe dig into my back. No matter how meticulous I was in packing the bag in a certain way, something pointy would always find its way through the other stuff to poke me. There would be a size-ten shoe stabbing me in the back, a deliberate metaphor reminding me of the excess I was carrying around the world. It's as though its purpose had evolved from fancy footwear to chief annoyer. It was a constant reminder that I had only worn those shoes once on this trip. Whilst we had no plans in Kranj, there was an opportunity to re-evaluate the baggage we were carrying and use the short time we had to maybe shed some weight. This would then help us get physically and mentally prepared for another long flight and a whole new culture in Myanmar before exploring the rest of Southeast Asia.

At each new hostel, the relief to unshackle myself from my belongings had increased as I almost wrestled the bag off my shoulders onto the cold hard floor. Our hostel in Kranj was pleasant enough as we found solace in the small room with cheap art above two single beds pushed together. Maybe because it was cold, wet, late and I was fatigued by the journey from Atlanta via Istanbul but, on that day, I threw much discontent towards my belongings. It got me so annoyed that it took some restraint to not use the bed as my top rope, shout a raspy "Ooooh Yeeahh!" and deliver a devastating elbow drop to the bag of stuff just like Macho Man Randy Savage. Hayley felt the same, but without a wrestling reference, as we agreed we were ready to discard some of the contents and send them the fuck home.

After breakfast, we returned to our room with one thing on our minds.

Less.

After thirty or so minutes unravelling the excess from the bags onto the bed we started to divide and conquer some of the items. Unrelenting, we created a pile of clothes, accessories, toiletries and shoes that had either not been worn yet or had rarely been used. Being caught up and consumed in the excitement of being in new clothing we had purchased from nearly everywhere we had been to date – California, Arizona, New Mexico, Texas, Louisiana, South Carolina, Florida – to remind us of those areas, but after each place, we quickly realised we didn't need those either. We were now being weighed down by stuff, old and new. We had superseded the other clothing with new go-to items. But as we moved from each new place to the next, we also started to leave old habits behind. The shift, or transformation, was observable. Our need for less items became more apparent. We replaced the need for physical things and souvenirs with the need for exploring and experiences instead.

It was time to let go.

I headed down to the hostel's reception thinking that they would have an empty box we could use but they had nothing of the sort. In an effort to be as helpful as possible, the receptionist gave me directions to a store that potentially sold boxes and proceeded to draw out a map of how to get there by foot. She spoke great English but between her lefts and rights, haphazard gesturing and the rough lines drawn with a blue biro, I became easily lost, but I kept smiling and nodding along anyway as only polite English people do. I managed to grab the name of the store and put it into Google maps, and it gave me a rough indication of where to head. The store was a twenty-minute walk away. Hayley and I grabbed our jackets and looked to seek out this mysterious shop in search of a large and sturdy cardboard box. We were living the dream.

What we were not told, nor did we anticipate, was that the twenty-minute walk was mostly downhill and would have taken that long had there not been ice on all the pavements and roads. In reality, the journey took three times longer, and was ten times as perilous. Here we were going on an icy expedition just to shop for a fucking empty box, holding on to each other and anything else we could grab on to as we slipped and slid our way down the road doing everything we could to avoid collapsing onto the floor.

Every now and then we saw another unfortunate soul hiking up the hill looking nervously as vans slowly made their way down the treacherous conditions. Brick walls and parked cars became our handrails as we carefully placed our wet trainers on the thickest part of the slush, each time making our bodies tense, bracing for a fall at any moment. It was as hilarious as it was terrifying. I often thought that if anybody had filmed us and put it on YouTube it would have gone viral immediately.

We arrived at the small industrial park about an hour later and entered the store. We were relieved that it had everything we needed, and we embraced the warmth of the inside, spending longer than average underneath the heater above the entrance. I quickly grabbed some masking tape and headed over to the aisle with the flat-packed cardboard boxes. The next few minutes were spent debating on what size box we should get, unfolding and folding back the boxes before placing them back on the shelf. Eventually, we decided we needed the biggest one available and headed to the counter. While paying for the box, I picked up some chocolate treats for us and to give to the hostel's receptionist for being so kind and helping us out.

Once out of the business park, we commenced our treacherous climb up the icy hill back to the hostel. I was holding a large flat-packed cardboard box under my arm and Hayley had a carrier bag of masking tape and tinned chocolate. The walk back took as long as the walk there. If it had been downhill, we could have used the box as a sledge, but alas it was all uphill.

Back at the hostel, I paraded our flat-pack purchase to the receptionist as if I'd won a trophy. She smiled and said, "Well done". She was surprised and delighted not only with the chocolate gift but also that we are still alive and in one piece.

The hero's quest to get the box became a teachable moment. The time it took to collect and the money it cost, and the stress it garnered, made us realise that our belongings still had the ability to get the better of us and impact our happiness despite us being 1,500 miles from home.

Without much hesitation, four pairs of shoes were thrown in on top of some ponchos we bought at Universal Studios Florida. Those ponchos cost $10 each. A purchase definitely where we were caught up in the magic of the park. Daylight robbery, if you ask me. The box was quickly filled with pairs of jeans, T-shirts, unworn shirts, dresses, trousers and tops. Some makeup also got thrown in there for good measure. There was little sentiment for what was going in the box, no "just in case" scenarios, no second-guessing. Our backpacks were left with just the essentials and they felt a lot lighter. I closed the box and tightly wrapped the tape around it, careful not to reduce the risk of the whole thing breaking and leaving our stuff who knows where on its way back to Hayley's mum's house. Ideally, we'd offload or donate the majority of the clothing, so we didn't really have the time or the local knowledge to make that happen, but we gave the all-clear for Hayley's mum to donate them to her local charity shop instead.

I carried the box out of the room and carefully walked down the narrow staircase, not really being able to see where I was going. Hayley and I kept shouting "PIVOT" to each other, referring to a classic *Friends* episode. As I turned a sharp corner, I caught my finger between the wall and the heavy box and pulled a face of anguish. The amount of minor pain my stuff had now caused me was unreal. I could feel a frustration creeping in.

Once downstairs we noticed the receptionist unwrapping some of the chocolates and she asked how we were before she gave us a thumbs up whilst she popped the treat in her mouth. The post office was not so far away but again we would have to navigate the icy pathways, just this time with a heavy box of crap.

As anticipated, the walk took us longer than we thought but the staff at the post office were friendly and walked us through everything we needed to do. It took us about fifteen minutes to fill out all the relevant forms, weigh the bloody stuff and then make a €40 payment to ship the package from Slovenia to the UK.

Whatever daylight there was had started to fade. Our only task had been completed and the stuff now was in the hands of the postal service. In truth, I didn't think either of us would have been that bothered if it got lost in transit.

All this extra stuff we'd been carrying around had become a nuisance. It felt like a lifetime ago I was sitting on the floor in my mum and dad's spare bedroom wrestling with the zips on the bag, trying forcefully to cram as much stuff as I could into it. Back then, the clothes and accessories still meant something to me. Not anymore. I'd rather pay to be rid of it all. The excess had caused an irritating back pain from the weight, slowed us down, become a source of frustration having to re-pack everything at each destination, wasted a whole day of our trip, and had hit our wallets as we sent the stuff back from whence it came. It was the next significant step in shedding stuff that added no value and was part of my soon-to-be former identity. Bye, Felicia! Good fucking riddance.

13. Striding Forwards

The 6am sunrise provided a breath-taking view of pink clouds mixed in with blue skies as far as the eye could see. The rolling landscape was still shrouded in twilight, but I just about made out the various greens and yellows of traditional agricultural farmland. The last sheet of dawn mist covered a small community of farmhouses into the distance. Swirls of off-white mixed with the rising sun in Kalaw on the morning of our fifty-seven kilometre, three-day, two-night trek across the Myanmar countryside. My eyes were not yet fully opened as they protected themselves from the glow offered outside but I dragged myself out of bed and took the few steps out onto the balcony of our hotel room to absorb the peaceful breeze as the day began to rise into action.

The weather predicted for the next three days was mild and cloudy with the odd bit of sunshine, perfect trekking weather. All we chose to take with us on the hike was a small backpack each that we carefully filled the night before we left with provisions needed for the seventy-two-hour trip. The bags were not filled to the brim, but included a couple of t-shirts rolled up, two changes of underwear, one pair of shorts, a couple of pairs of socks, snacks, our water bottles and a very small first-aid kit for impending blisters, back aches and other sore muscles that we were bound to get. There was one toiletries bag that included our toothbrushes, toothpaste, some sun cream and of course, the most essential item of all, hair wax. Even in the sparse countryside, I still needed to tend to the barnet. It had grown a little wild and gnarly having only had one haircut the whole time we'd been away, which was in a small barbershop in Lafayette, Louisiana. I was forced to wear hair bands at times to get it out of my face. We also packed cash and phones, of which mine now had a crack in the bottom right-hand corner after sitting on a wall with it in my back pocket in Tampa.

Once we were showered and ready to leave yet another bed behind (our thirty-eighth, but who's counting?) we took our two large backpacks and our smaller trek backpacks down to reception and checked out of our hotel. We left the four bags in the corner by the reception desk and strolled over to the dining room where a light breakfast buffet of bread, cereal and fruit was on offer. We anticipated a lot of walking, so we quickly gorged on bananas, watermelon and a couple of slices of toast alongside a scattering of other weary guests, who were taking their time with their cups of tea. We stole a couple more bananas for the road and wandered back out to sit in reception. We were due to meet our guide, Sithu, who would meet us here and had arranged for our somewhat lighter large bags to be picked up and taken to the next hotel we were staying at near Inle Lake, a great touch and a welcome respite from lugging them around.

Whilst waiting for him to arrive I admired the décor in the middle of the reception as a sad-looking skinny Christmas tree reached all the way up to the ceiling. The tree was draped in green and blue tinsel as well as a random assortment of small soft toys, different-coloured ribbons and sparkling baubles. Small fairy lights were wrapped around the almost dead tree, but they had yet to be switched on. At the base of the tree was a bunch of boxes of different sizes wrapped up in bright pinks, blues and gold paper. Some were plain and some had flowers and hearts on. Sitting on the boxes was more tinsel, silver this time, party hats, paper bells, cotton wool, which I guess was to represent snow, and of course a two-foot stuffed toy of the man of the moment, Santa Claus himself, who was looking rather jolly, arms out-stretched. We were still a few weeks away from the big day but in Myanmar, the festivities started from December 1st, which is also known as 'Sweet December' by the young and old.

My inquisitive gaze at the boxes, wondering if they were empty or not, was broken by the engine sound of a moped driving up to the reception doors. As I anticipated the arrival of our guide, two guys came strolling in and they immediately clocked us. We couldn't look more like tourists today, huge bags within arm's reach, ruffled and messy hair and clunky bright-coloured running trainers. We stuck out like sore thumbs, waiting to be taken on our next adventure. Although full of anticipation, some of it was slightly mixed as we weren't a hundred per cent sure of the itinerary. We roughly knew that for the next three days we'd be walking loads with maybe a couple of breaks in between and then sleeping in local villages, but we didn't know all the details. We didn't know the timings, the size of the trekking group, the types of food we'd get, the terrain, who we'd stay with, but that was OK now. We had acclimatised to being comfortable with the uncomfortable, the known unknown.

"Chris, Hayley?" the slightly taller guy of the duo asked excitedly as he waved us over. "I'm your guide, Sithu. Are you ready to go?"

We greeted Sithu with a warm handshake.

Sithu was exactly Hayley's height, about five-foot-six and slender. His black baseball cap was on backwards and he was dressed in a baggy white t-shirt. Sithu's friend, who was a little shorter but had a distinct blond streak in his black hair, gave us a big smile, and paced over to our large bags. In one swift movement, he grabbed both of them and put one on each of his shoulders as he paced out of the hotel, slightly dragged down by our stuff, and expertly tied them on to the back of his bike. He would have had to drag them along the floor if we'd not lightened the load in Kranj. It's here that I realised how useless all that other clothing really was. Here we were about to go out into the wilderness, and all we really needed was the essentials.

"Your stuff will meet you at your next hotel," Sithu reassured us. We did know that was happening, but the surgical approach was a bit of a shock. I got that tense uncomfortable feeling again of letting go but I was happy our bags had gone, if only for a few days. Without them being in my eyeline, I felt lighter. I focused on what I had in front of me, not what was on my back, behind me.

The sun did its best to greet us on our first few steps on the dirt track, but it remained shy, behind the thick clouds. Leading the way, our guide broke a few gooseberries off a bush and snacked on them as he rearranged his own backpack. I copied him as I guessed they were safe to eat, and pulled a face due to the sourness. Hayley did the same as we chuckled behind Sithu. He smiled when he realised that we'd thrown a few in our mouth, like he had. The path got thinner as we walked past rickety fences looking out on to the vast green hills as they climbed into the clouds. A handful of shacks and different-coloured rooftops scattered the greenery as Sithu explained each one was likely to be farmers growing their crops on the steep hills. Each step felt effortless as the wonder of being in the open countryside learning about the landscape from our guide overtook any early tiredness.

Within a few hours we came to a more built-up area and passed through a village where we saw two other travellers on a tandem bike, the only non-locals we saw the whole time we were trekking. The cyclists attracted a small group of kids from the local monastery and they were determined to ride on the bikes with them. As we stopped to take a drink, the kids got their wish as one of them, wearing maroon robes with a shaven head, climbed on to the back seat and started to pedal around in circles with the traveller, as his partner leant up against a rock drinking from a bottle of water. The kids all laughed and pointed, running after the bike, getting enjoyment from these visitors. I'm sure those guys would have had to give every kid a go. I asked Sithu what the red robes represented, and he responded, "Simplicity and detachment from materials," which I interpreted as material possessions.

An interesting connection as we couldn't be more detached from the world, and yet paradoxically be right in the middle of it. No phone signal and minimal belongings on our person. The kids, who may not have had regular access to the internet or video games, found entertainment in the simplest of things, like riding a bike, and it was a beautiful thing to witness.

Before I could think too deeply, another half a dozen local children came running around the corner as a further two travellers on mountain bikes appeared and connected with the two adults that were already here. Child monks and local kids were now gathering in groups around each of the bikes, desperate to have a go, and the travellers were keen to help each one up onto the saddle and push them along. We laughed and smiled along with the other adults taking a break from riding as Sithu led us on down the hill and around the corner to our first official stop at a small and isolated home overlooking amazing valley peaks and troughs in various shades of green, displaying carefully planted trees and harvested lands. Two cups of warm tea were immediately brought out of the little shack and placed on a makeshift bamboo table to the right of the small family home. Sithu informed us that we would stop here for half an hour for some food and explained that the owner of the home and the immediate land grew ginger. As we took a load off and relaxed, drinking our tea overlooking the beautiful landscape, a moped turned up and I recognised it as the bike guy that took our bags a few hours earlier. The driver gave us a quick wave as he unloaded a small bag and took in a single pot to cook with. Within a few minutes Sithu brought out bowls of carefully cut mango, salad and homemade chapatis. My stomach yearned for these fresh delights as it let out a menacing growl that I tried to mask by stretching my arms and taking an over-the-top deep breath.

The guy on the bike, whose name we found out later was Amah, was also the chef and swiftly followed with bowls of noodle dishes, fried rice and pancakes. It all looked fantastic and we started to pick from each dish slowly, taking in all the tastes and appreciating the brilliance of it all. All put together so simply but presented so elegantly. Hayley and I laughed at how much kitchenware we had previously invested in and we vowed that when we returned, would jettison as much remaining kitchenware as we could. Sandwich makers remained redundant, excess pots were left at the back of cupboards and well-intended pans moved further and further away from any prepping area. The quality of our dishes was nothing compared to what we had eaten but it was just another example of the perception that more meant better.

Sithu advised we were making good time so there was no

rush as he disappeared back into the shack and left us to just be. There were no emails to check, no texts to respond to, no timelines to catch up on, it was just us, good food and the unpolluted rural air. A slight haze softened our view across the valleys when a breeze came through as the dust kicked up from the tracks created by years of necessary agricultural trade back and forth. We saw buffalo in the distance led by ladies from the Shan state carrying fresh ginger, peanuts and chillies. Daily life was happening around us and we were grateful to peer into it, unspoilt by tourism, machinery and interference. In that moment, the life I left meant nothing and I just let the landscape naturally imprint on my eyes. I stayed in this hypnotic, peace-filled state for two days. I had no cares in the world, except for the one beneath my feet.

As we completed our trek on day three, we rested our weary bodies, feet and legs tired from the walk and bellies full from the many feasts. Hayley showed me a picture she'd taken whilst we were in a tearoom at a train station platform we stopped at. It was of me and she referred to the smile on my face, one she had not seen this big for some time. Teeth on display, cheeks higher up by my eyes, I looked so happy. Completely in my element. In that one picture, I had little concept of time, I was in no rush. I had not been distracted with pings and bleeps. My mind and senses were computing the new tastes of different tea, the smells, the people, our simple but challenging quest, the fresh air, the views of beautiful landscape, and it all came out of me in this big smile. Content.

I never once thought about the stuff left in the bags awaiting us at our next hotel. I completely forgot about it all. Every new step on difficult terrain, avoiding uneven surfaces, making small adjustments, twisting and turning, was a step forward and another small step away from a lifestyle of hustle consumed by things and busyness. I hadn't used my phone (other than to take pictures) for three days. Three days offline, that was unheard of. Three hours would have been a push just a few months prior.

This new culture, an adventure within an adventure, helped

me reinvent myself. It made me more open to different ways of thinking, different perspectives even. Because I had to focus on learning how to approach brand-new situations and navigate new experiences, it gave me a new level of fulfilment. Adam Galinsky from Columbia Business School said that visiting a foreign place and immersing yourself in the local environment increases your cognitive flexibility and depth of thought as well as boosting creativity. He also added that extended travelling improves productivity, problem solving and the probability of getting a promotion or pay rise at work. Sweet. Well, what I can tell you all now by connecting the dots is that in the two and a half years since returning from travelling in February 2018, my income has increased by 52 per cent. In the ten years previous it increased 1 to 2 per cent each year if I was lucky. I'm not driven financially but money does sit in the car. We all have bills to pay, so if you were looking for a bump in income to supplement any clutter you sell off, and drawing a pretty nifty line graph, taking an extended break to a foreign land could be the best way to do it.

There was no gift shop at the end of this ride, no souvenirs to purchase, no mementos to put on a shelf or a fridge to remind me of this trek. A few pictures and a bucket-load of memories were all the souvenirs I needed. The memories were in me now forever. And rather than weigh me down – they would pick me up.

14. Minimalism? What's That?

It was just getting light outside when I was woken early by a strange noise of shuffling, heavy breathing and snorting. No, it was not Hayley in one of her deep-sleep stages, it was right outside our small, but perfectly sized ecolodge. Our latest stop-off was in the Ninh Bình province of Vietnam. It was a pretty unspoilt area and there weren't that many tourists knocking about. Other than the confusing early morning cacophony, it was quiet, tranquil and an ideal location for a short stay to recharge after day-long bus rides and busy cities.

I did all I could to reach out of the bed to pull the curtain slightly so I could cast my bleary eyes and investigate where these noises were coming from. If I was able to keep the majority of my body in the warm under the covers, everything would be alright regardless of any threats. "Keep your feet under the covers so the monsters under the bed don't get you," that type of thinking. To my surprise and wonder, a herd of six pigs meandered around on the grass outside, barely two metres from our glass sliding doors. The teamwork looked good and they didn't spend too long in one area, clearly knowing the patch and where to find some good breakfast treats. Although I was two-thirds still in the bed, reaching over my now half-empty backpack, I was stretching to keep the curtain open and grab my phone so I could capture some video. I did all I could to keep as still as possible so as not to startle our visitors. They started feeding on a few bits and pieces in and around the trees, I could only guess they had found some insects and were enjoying their meal. Their noses took them further away from the lodge and into longer grass and they'd not looked up once to see where they were going. Straight across pathways and wetter, more dense terrain, their noses were definitely leading the way and I'd been completely ignored.

Next to the trees and where the pigs had wandered off to was a small bridge, which acted as the quickest route to the base of the Hang Mua peak. Strolling across the bridge like he owned the place was a loud and obnoxious rooster who had been waking everyone up since 5am. I knew he'd be a problem as soon as we checked in. Within a few seconds of him crowing, Hayley started to wake and released a huff of annoyance as she turned on her side to try and ignore the noise. All the activity outside had well and truly woken me. Nature had woken me. It couldn't be any further from the TV alarm and breakfast TV presenters that broke me out of my slumber every morning in London. I did miss Andi Peters though, oddly. I couldn't tell you if he still gives his gun show and competition combo every morning. I hope so. I certainly never won his text giveaway competition any of the multiple times I played.

Hayley and I's approach to tackling the growing list of things to do in each place had slowed recently too. We were OK with missing out on some things so we could enjoy the activities we invested our time and energy in. There had been a couple of occasions where we tried to fit lots into limited time only to then be absolutely wiped at our next destination. On that particular January morning, we were getting out early, earlier than planned because of the fucking rooster, and looking to achieve two things: a walk to neighbouring Trang An to enjoy a peaceful rowing boat trip meandering through beautiful scenery, temples and mysterious caves, followed by scaling the 500 steps to the top of Hang Mua peak.

Our hour-long walk to the boats was through villages and even though the day was a little cloudy, we took in the lush green scenery and smiled back at locals going about their daily routine. A few tourists cycled past us heading to the same destination, but we were quite content taking our time. The boat ride was fantastic and we both enjoyed feeling like we were guests of nature, being one of only a few people out that day. All the rowers were female, and they asked us where we were from by pointing to themselves and saying, "Vietnam," and then pointing at us so we could do the same. They smiled and giggled to each other as we carefully stepped back onto their boats, keeping our balance and trying not to fall into the water. Our walk back to our ecolodge was only interrupted by Hayley stepping in dog shit, which I immediately recorded a video of as she scraped her trainer on the grass. I very much enjoyed the travelling experience of seeing amazing scenery one minute and then stepping in dog turds the next. It kept it all real.

Following our time on the water, we strolled past our lodge and over the small bridge to the base of the Mua Cave mountain. The rooster was nowhere in sight, probably napping. Bastard.

We began our ascent up the large stone staircase and passed other visitors struggling their way going up and also see the smug faces coming back down. Each step upwards was slightly more difficult and different from the last, either by size or shape, some required more effort than others, but it was definitely working the calves. Every fifty steps or so we stopped to rehydrate and took in the view of rice paddy fields and the Ngô Đồng river winding through Tam Coc. The waterway weaved itself like a snake through the yellowy-green ripening fields at the base of limestone mountains.

It wasn't an easy trek and it didn't take long for the humidity and exertion to bring a sweaty brow and aching muscles. It took us about forty-five minutes to reach the summit and we really appreciated the sights beneath us. Also, at the highest viewpoint was the lying dragon, a superb little pavilion and a small handful of people taking selfies and aiming to get that perfect pic for the 'gram. It was almost like there was a queue to get that ideal picture and that became their goal rather than reaching the top and then just taking it in. I'm not against taking pictures and the culture of "doing it for Insta'," but on that occasion, Hayley and I took a couple of shots and just tried to be present, absorbing the achievement, being in the moment and enjoying the view.

Our use of social media in general changed and evolved during the Asia part of our tour. We hadn't completely detoxed from the apps but our use of them reduced heavily. Because we never really knew exactly what we were going to do most days, we spent most of our online time researching local areas, reading about things we had seen, heard or experienced and paving our way forward with maps and directions. I learnt how to say a few phrases in each country we went to so I could at least take part in some kind of conversation. We did however understand that there were a lot of people back home that were following our journey, like our families and friends, who wanted to stay updated with what we got up to. My mum and dad especially liked knowing we were safe by us posting pictures regularly, so we had to make sure that we checked in with those responsibilities on our down time. I deleted the LinkedIn app on a train from Toronto to Montréal, out of spite, in many ways, because a random message from someone trying to sell me something interrupted me reading *The Girl with the Dragon Tattoo*. Notifications from Facebook, Twitter and the others were all switched off too after a blast of messages came through in the middle of the night one time because of the time differences, so the twitch to check them all the time had significantly minimised. They had fallen way down the pecking order, so they became a little trivial when we were out exploring.

Half-an-hour or so later, the sun started to set on another excellent day in Vietnam and we returned to the base of the mountain. Our feet were a little sore and I got those distinct back sweat patches where I'd been carrying the backpack. It was a bit rank, but they tended to be an indication that we'd had a productive day of adventuring. It wasn't long before night surrounded us, and the place went eerily quiet. No more visitors, no pigs, certainly no rooster, just a couple of dim lights indicating a pathway to the reception. We had totally earned our dinner followed by bed and film night, a weary traveller's version of Netflix and Chill. Bed and film night was exactly what you would expect, watching a film whilst relaxing in bed, probably whilst eating a ton of foreign snacks.

The iPad we had brought with us had been invaluable for being that multipurpose bit of tech where we could read, listen to music, watch films, play puzzles and stay connected with friends and family whilst moving from place to place. We were also booking things as we went along, effectively living day to day. Luckily, the ecolodge had acceptable Wi-Fi so we had an opportunity to peruse the latest options on Netflix.

Hayley spent ten minutes swiping left and right to find the optimum film for us to watch, something we could probably both tolerate. The ultimate compromise.

Down the Netflix rabbit hole, she selected one film and handed me the tablet.

Minimalism: A documentary about the important things.

"Fancy that?" she asked.

I read the blurb that accompanied the film to see if it piqued my catalogue of interests.

"People dedicated to rejecting the American ideal that things bring happiness are interviewed in this documentary showing the virtues of less is more."

"Sounds interesting," I said. "I've never heard of minimalism but yep, I'm up for that,"

The documentary had been available on UK Netflix for a whole year prior to this but we had never spotted it. We were too engrossed watching *Stranger Things* and *Game of Thrones*.

With the film selection made (usually it takes more time than the length of a film), we then really turned up the comfort level: cups of tea were made, water bottles were replenished, and lighting was adjusted. Now we were in peak chill mode. I hit play and turned the volume up to an acceptable level, Hayley then turned it down a bit.

Within the first minute we were presented with waves of people outside a department store in the US, rushing to get in to grab whatever deal they possibly could. The clip cut to a group of people fighting with each other over a heavily discounted flatscreen TV. It looked like people were rioting and looting, but it became clear that it was something like a Black Friday sales event.

"Fucking hell," we both yelled, whilst simultaneously shaking our heads.

I was hooked.

Then, this guy appeared on the screen with long brown hair, a bit of a hippy vibe. My hair and beard were pretty wild at that time, so I appreciated his look. On his feet were what looked like pieces of cardboard held together by string. He then walked outside, stepped on his skateboard and rode off onto the road, weaving in and out of traffic.

He then just dropped truth bomb after truth bomb.

"I was attempting to buy my way to happiness. I had everything I was supposed to have. I was spending money faster than I was earning it," he said.

That line resonated with me immediately. It ping-ponged between my ears.

"Eventually happiness had to be somewhere around the corner. I was living paycheck to paycheck. Living for a paycheck, living for stuff – but I wasn't really living at all."

Holy shit.

The guy with the long hair and cardboard shoes was Ryan Nicodemus, he was one half of The Minimalists, America's minimalist movement ringleaders, as described by *New York Magazine*. Within seconds I related to him, and his best friend and other half of the duo, Joshua Fields Millburn, as well as the rest of the people we were introduced to within the first five minutes of the film.

I watched and listened intently as each author, economist, entrepreneur, neuropsychologist and architect shared their story of reaching a point in life before deciding to effectively live a new life. How? By ditching all their stuff. The pull-through of the movie seemed to be that a major traumatic event or a collection of smaller negative events impacted these people's lives, which then prompted them to re-evaluate everything they had ever known, or at least ever purchased. I guessed those events, tragic or trivial, was when these people knew they had reached a crossroads. Only then did they feel able to choose a new path.

The less-is-more message was powerful.

I was inspired.

I sat up straight and leant in towards the iPad. I wanted to shake it so that it would spill even more information.

Halfway through the film, I started to connect what these guys were saying to some of my own practices leading up to that point. The large backpack that then held the majority of my life was on the floor by the bed, its contents significantly reduced as the trip had gone on; however, when we first started it was super-heavy and included excess that we just didn't use or need.

Click.

Yes, I heard things in my head click into place.

Everything I had done in the past few months leading up to that point were all connected. Selling the DVDs, the irrational emotional attachment, ditching even more possessions, taking a career break, letting go of limits, finding more motivation and energy by doing less, stepping out of my comfort prison and confronting the fear of the unknown. The stuff that I clung on to so tightly was actually the stuff that was suffocating me and holding me back from moving forwards. Everything that felt strange and different but empowering, it all had a name.

Minimalism.

Mic drop.

The lifestyle presented to me in this film focused on the important things, whatever that was, to us individually. It was the pursuit of living a meaningful life... with less. I resonated with it immediately – the dots were no longer just dots; they were a network of points all connected together. I felt like Neo at the end of *The Matrix* (which ironically was the one DVD boxset I struggled to get rid of the most) – I understood everything.

The documentary makers spoke of being intentional and having control. I felt that when I was making tough decisions about my own life in advance of the trip. They spoke about simplicity. Again, I felt that same feeling during the last few months by focusing on creating money and opportunities, rather than wasting them. I called it curating the journey.

Right then, as I sat in the hotel bed brushing crumbs off myself after snacking on some weird foreign crisps, I was bang in the middle of minimalism. This was what we were doing. We were the epitome of what they labelled as minimalists. We had removed the excess from our lives and were living better with less. A lot less! We were in an amazing country, far away from everything we had ever known, we had limited funds, our backpacks and each other, but that was all we needed. We were making the most of the resources we had. We were collecting memories and life-changing experiences, not things.

All those feelings and thoughts I had whilst decluttering my life in London, the shift in mindset from drifting in my career to taking ownership and the subsequent actions following all of that I could now package up into this whole new "minimalism" lifestyle. And it was so comforting to see those guys point the way.

The documentary ended and I stood up and paced the room. Hayley was fast asleep, as she so often was within minutes of watching a movie. In that room, at that moment, my mind was whizzing with ideas and thoughts. Finally, I could put a name to all the things I'd been feeling and doing. It was a rush. I was no longer lost. I had found my people. I was a minimalist.

"We should have stayed here longer," Hayley said as she pulled her backpack over her shoulders.

"Yep," I responded, bending down looking underneath the bed, making sure we hadn't forgotten anything, a habit ingrained in me since leaving an expensive plug adapter in a San Antonio hotel.

It was another early start as we strolled out of our lodge in Ninh Bình, refreshed and, for me in particular, renewed. The air was a mixture of humidity and morning freshness. We walked side by side down a dusty dirt track looking across at the farmworkers toiling away in the rice paddies. The distinctive conical bamboo hats shielded the workers from any rays of anticipated sunlight. The huge limestone rocks and mountains beyond them were dressed in January fog, which would start to clear over the next few hours. I pulled in a big breath, pushed my shoulders back and slowly let the air out. A good start to a new year, I thought. Just ten days prior, we had celebrated the introduction of 2018 with colourful fireworks at an event in Vientiane, Laos, but those fireworks were now in my head. I was miles away from anywhere I had ever been before, physically and mentally, and that fact – coupled with the minimalism revelation – made me feel good. We had one final opportunity to absorb the tranquillity of the place before being interrupted by exhaust fumes spitting out the back of the small bus that would return us to Hanoi airport, part one of two that transported us south to our next destination, Hue. I took the two steps up into the bus and banged my head on the door frame. At the same time, my phone vibrated in my back pocket.

We found a spot at the back of the bus, a place I always gravitated to in my teens, and my knees pushed up against the seat in front. Our bags were squeezed into the overhead compartment – as they now had less in them, they were easier to manipulate. The three-hour ride was a tight squeeze so I got out the Kindle and my phone and slid them underneath my legs; there would be no way of shuffling things in and out of bags for a while. Once we were on the move, I unlocked my phone with my fingerprint, and I saw my brother had sent me five photos via WhatsApp. It took a second to comprehend what it was, but I quickly identified my mum and dad's driveway and easily recognised both their cars. Next to the cars on the driveway was a silver BMW on its roof, windows smashed in and covered in shrubbery.

A wave of WTF submerged me.

Instinctively, my toes curled, and my body went stiff. My breathing turned quick and shallow.

I swiped left. The next picture showed skid marks on the road and debris from the pathway. Branches from a nearby tree were strewn all over the pavement and onto the gravel. Before I let my mind start to create its own outcomes, I continued to swipe. The third picture was a close-up of my dad's old Nissan, the rear bumper had been cracked and one of the tyres was deflated. A small dent was in my mum's red Peugeot and my dad was standing in the background with his hands in his pockets. He looked fine. My brother had sent only images, so my worried mind tried to piece the scene together.

The next photo was from another angle and showed the silver BMW being dragged out of the driveway by a tow truck. Red and white cones were lined up outside cornering off a part of the road, two men in orange high-vis jackets stood by. It appeared as if bits of bodywork from the BMW had fallen off as it was dragged away from the scene. A mangled wing mirror and bits of glass were everywhere. The front-left wheel was at a different angle than the rest indicating that the heaviest of damage was done on the passenger side. The axle appeared to have come away and the underneath of the car looked messed up, but I am no vehicle expert. Stuff looked out of place, but I couldn't say what was what. In the background of the picture on the other side of the road was a red convertible BMW, the driver, clearly visible, was taking a nice long look at the damage. People just can't resist slowing down and getting a glimpse of an accident, can they? They won't slow down for their own lives, but they will to see the possible end of someone else's.

"What the fuck has happened?" I thought to myself repeatedly. I showed Hayley the photos.

The final image was of my car, a navy-blue 2000 Vauxhall Vectra, shunted against a fence. The back of it had virtually collapsed, the registration plate was on the floor, bent and covered in red glass. The lights on the right side were caved in and the boot was half open. Fence panels leant up against the car and pieces of wood were scattered around the bumper, which was hanging by a thread. A dark-grey piece of metal lay next to the rear-right tyre and I couldn't for the life of me tell what part of a car that was from. It was an absolute mess. A car crash, you could say.

As Hayley swiped through the photos, my brother sent a message confirming everyone was OK, the time delay had clearly been him writing a bumper message. His text suggested that the morning before a young lad had been speeding down the road outside my parent's house, lost control of his car, hit a kerb and flipped it against a tree and smashed into the cars on my mum and dad's driveway. Surprisingly, no one was injured, not even the driver, who apparently just opened the door and crawled out with a couple of scratches. My parents then invited him into their house for a cup of tea whilst the police and ambulance turned up. It was only by chance that my brother was driving past in the morning on his way to work and saw the damage. He pulled up and went into the house to check on everyone but had an opportunity to speak to the driver whilst my parents were outside calculating the damage. The driver had apparently been speeding at 85mph on a 30mph residential road because "there was no other traffic". That was it. He wasn't under the influence of anything, wasn't late, he just felt like blasting down the street.

"Your car is gone," my brother wrote in his message. Thankfully, he didn't follow it up with a sad face emoji.

The car was on its last legs anyway. It had been declared off the road, or SORN (So Old Right Now), and had started to cough and splutter its way through most journeys before we had even left the driveway. Before we left, I thought it would be a good idea to store it on my parents' driveway, so we had an option to get it repaired and use it when we got back. In truth, it should have been scrapped way before then, but my mindset was to just keep hold of it and allow it to take up room next to the other cars, stuck in the corner, unused and unloved. It was another "just in case" item that someone else had to take care of in my absence.

Obliterated and written off, the car was just another thing I had to let go of. The difference this time was that it was completely out of my control. I wasn't actually that fussed about it, I said to Hayley, maybe even a little pleased it happened. One less thing for me to remove from my life. I anticipated some upset or emotional attachment but there was nothing there. The car was just one more thing that was part of life before travel, before growth, before discovering what minimalism was. Call it coincidence, irony or fate, but that incident was just another indication that when we returned, we could choose to live more intentionally and not be held back by items of the past. Maybe we didn't need a car, maybe we'd ride bikes, maybe we'd take advantage of rentals and taxis, who knows, but whatever we decided, it would be done with purpose.

After a few hours calculating our remaining budget during some down time in Nha Trang, we decided that Vietnam would be the final stop on our tour as money was starting to dwindle away. We could see the conclusion to this journey on the horizon we were determined to not make this the only time we take this type of adventure or time out. We arranged one final flight, the one to take us home, from Singapore for a few weeks' time and that gave us our new end date. Six weeks earlier than originally planned but we were OK with that. Not only would my parents be pleased that we were coming back a few weeks early, but we'd also spend some down time back in London to reflect and really think about what was next. The end of this tour was only the beginning of something else. I knew that now.

This whole journey had given me more than I could ever have wished for. I learnt that I didn't need to organise things within an inch of its life to enjoy the adventures. At times, we were literally planning the next place to sleep as we were driving towards it.

Interestingly, the bigger my beard grew, the more drugs I got offered.

Work wasn't on my mind after the first few weeks. I was officially on annual leave in Denmark, Slovenia and up until we hit Toronto, but once I had no more salary coming in, I felt detached from it. I started to ponder a little bit about what a future career would look like at the back end of Vietnam.

I reconnected with my childhood and had the best time at Universal Studios in Orlando, and I'd go again, and again! Hayley had never been to any sort of theme park on this scale, so it was great to experience that with her.

I found that when you step purposefully and confidently into uncomfortable and unknown situations, it rewards you with a new level of awareness and growth. Whenever we found ourselves lost in the woods or on the road, which was many times, we always found our way back. There was one specific time I remember getting really angry about going way off course whilst trekking around Kings Canyon National Park in California's Sierra Nevada mountains. Notable for its absolutely massive sequoia trees (General Sherman, the largest known living single stemmed tree on earth was nearby), we spent most of the hike looking up at them and of course, got fucking lost. All alone in this huge national park, I started to panic about bears and strolling on to random bits of private land where someone would shoot first and ask questions later. We ended up walking towards the sound of cars driving by and climbed over a fence back onto the highway and subsequently walking on the road for just over a mile and a half. I even flipped the bird at the National Park road sign as I bounded forward in a huff back towards the parking lot. Hayley filming me and laughing behind my back at my strange decision to throw my full frustrated energy at a road sign helped me come down from my irrational place. Once the anger at myself and the poor innocent sign subsided, I realised there were worse places to get lost and actually it was a funny and poignant story I could probably use in a book someday. Generally, whenever we got lost, the story of finding our way back was a little more interesting.

Whenever we were faced with problems, such as arriving at our Airbnb in New Orleans that was infested with insects and not safe to stay in, we had the courage to challenge and call out the bullshit and then react quickly to make alternative arrangements. Before, I would have likely tolerated it to avoid any conflict.

Being a city boy, I took nature for granted, so the time spent being present within spectacular surroundings made me appreciate tranquillity. Nature was good for the soul and I hadn't really acknowledged that until the trip. It felt like a great antidote to the overwhelming consumption and consumerism of a busy modern life. It's something that would become far more important in my daily routine moving forwards.

Once we started to run out of money, we had to make a choice. We set ourselves a budget and when we started to get near it, we discussed the option of carrying on and dipping into our savings, which we had considered setting aside for our next deposit on a new home. We felt ending on a high in Vietnam was a good place to stop. We had achieved what we wanted to and carried enough motivation into life back home. Like me, Hayley felt rejuvenated, like a new person. This was now the new priority, doing this. Exploring, living, going on adventures, trying new things. Together we would not be held down by our old mindsets and perceptions on what we are supposed to do.

How about now, slowed down yet?

There were many stops on our journey but for this story there were pivotal ones that illuminated my minimalist mindset. San Francisco, where the wishing tree highlighted to me that I needed to stop the mental clutter. In Sedona, I did finally stop. In Slovenia I shed more stuff and in Myanmar I fully shed my old identity. I learnt from my trip that I didn't need a lot of stuff to experience the best bits of life. I saw first-hand how in certain cultures, such as Laos, working and earning money are not prioritised, even in the capital Vientiane and the beautiful Luang Prabang. The simple life was valued there. You worked to live, not lived to work. Eating well, drinking, relaxing and peace was something that stood out with locals along the Mekong River. It was a variation on the hustle we were both accustomed to back home. I learnt that, in the end, everything was going to be OK and that the challenges we faced and resilience we showed to overcome them just added to the story. A minimalist's story.

PHASE FOUR

A New Normal

"If you don't design your career or prioritise your life, someone else will do it for you."
Greg McKeown, *Essentialism: The Disciplined Pursuit of Less*

15. Home

As the plane descended through the dark clouds and dreary London skies, I struggled to swallow down saliva in an attempt to make my ears pop to counter the change in air pressure. With my hearing muffled, I opened my mouth for longer than normal, and moved my jaw from left to right to encourage a fake yawn. That did the trick.

Water droplets danced across the windows either side of me; each bead followed the same path of the one before running in the slip stream but never able to catch up. My neck grinded and clicked as I stretched in my seat looking around at all the weary passengers, trying to catch a glimpse of daylight out the window.

By clenching my butt cheeks and wiggling my toes, I started to wake up parts of my body that had themselves been in flight mode in preparation for standing up, moving on and carrying my bloody backpack one final time. Unable to have found any sort of consistent sleep, fifteen hours in the air felt like days. The in-flight entertainment had done its best to keep me occupied but my mind had been on overdrive the entire flight; I was anxious for my feet to feel solid ground. Even though I'd been on dozens of flights in the last few months, turbulence still made me sweat a little. The black mirror a foot in front of my face had switched off and I caught a glimpse of myself reflecting back in the darkness. I looked like a bag of shit. My hair was unkempt and uncut and accompanied by a massive beard which had grown downwards as well as outwards, leaning more to the right as I tried to smooth it down. I told Hayley on our first day away that I wanted to just let it grow. Fuck it, I thought, let's see what would happen. It was a slight attitude adjustment reminiscent of trying to make my own rules with that feeling of being freer, wilder even. I'd started to use my hair wax on the beard to tame it a little. Over the last few months, I'd developed a habit of stroking the face fuzz and grooming it with my fingers, like some kind of shaman about to offer some wisdom. It had become like an unconscious twitch and I kept having to snap back out of a daze and put my hand down by my side. Although I may have given off the traditional impression that I was pondering a thought deep and meaningful whilst twisting and twirling the ends of my moustache, the majority of the time I had no idea I was even doing it. I was simply away with the fairies, daydreaming. As much as I had enjoyed my face companion, I fantasised about walking into a barber's and getting it removed within the next few days. Interestingly, my out-of-control beard and excessive mop on my head was reminiscent of how my mind used to be, fuzzy, disorganised and unkempt. I wanted to declutter my face and make it a parallel to my new state of mind.

In between all the amazing experiences of travelling were the moments of down time. There was plenty of waiting before flights, waiting around for buses, days lingering in hotel rooms and long journeys from one destination to another with little else to do but sit and stare out of the window, think, and daydream. They were pockets of time where there were limits to what you could do. Sometimes there was no puzzle to solve, no FaceTime or Skype calls, no parks to visit, no people to watch. You were just there, being. It took me a few months to fully learn how to enjoy doing nothing and to stop propelling my mind into action mode. Boredom, to me, was always connected to negativity: being bored would give me the hump, a restriction placed on me because I didn't have enough gadgets or things to do to keep me on the go. What I learnt during my travels was that it was OK to get bored. One day I wasn't in the mood to read or mindlessly check Twitter, so I researched about boredom instead. In *National Geographic*, I read an article that said that when the mind wanders, different parts of our brain become active, checking in on areas and information that may have lain dormant. It went on to say that it increased creativity, insights of wisdom and often solutions to problems that the person had not considered. So actually, it was probably good for me. Not long after reading that, I spent an hour trying to get a small cookie from my forehead into my mouth using only my face muscles whilst lying down. This task was not as easy as you might have thought, as the nose will invariably get in the way and take the confectionery off course; however, the time spent daydreaming sent me into exploratory mode about myself and how I wanted to show up in the future. It was also an opportunity to give my brain a rest from the constant stimulation of adventure. All those smells, tastes, sights and cultures that were absorbed on an almost daily basis was, at times, quite overwhelming, so it gave me the opportunity to stop letting the world in. I unplugged.

The pilot's calming voice lifted us all gently out of our various forms of slumber and welcomed us to the UK. He relayed the estimated arrival time and, begrudgingly, the temperature of eight degrees Celsius, which was followed by a few typically British groans from passengers in our immediate vicinity. What may have been an uneventful landing at Gatwick airport on an overcast Wednesday morning for most, was actually the start of a new chapter for me. There was no sadness or bitterness in returning, in fact, quite the opposite. I was riding on the high of smashing out of the safe and low-risk comfort zone, through the fear, through the learning, facing challenges and problem solving all the way through to the growth zone, living the dream of sorts, finding purpose and conquering goals. I'd lived a catalogue of experiences that I would remember forever: the trek in Myanmar, absorbing nature in California, driving through Texas, our friends' weddings in Jamaica and Slovenia, all of Vietnam, cycling through Laos, they were just a few. I was now confident that I could take on the world while at the same time incredibly grateful for all the people we met and things we encountered on the way. I was now Chris Lovett in ultra-high definition. A 4D Chris, if you will.

Upon touchdown, our plan moving forward was to stay at my parents' house for a few months whilst we got back into the swing of things.

Whilst, there was no welcome party upon our arrival, back at my parents' house there were huge hugs and big smiles, which was more than enough. Still giddy with excitement, we told them stories from our adventures and enjoyed home-cooked meals, the first transition back into "real life", as my dad kept repeating. I sensed he was anxious about what we had planned next. I was just excited. I also sensed that my parents had noticed a change in me – more than just my outward appearance. Intertwined into all the storytelling were queries around future plans – "What next?"

The types of questions we were now asking each other had evolved from the carefree to the more profound.

What did I want to achieve?

Where did we want to live?

What were we going to do now?

These questions had superseded the previous one of "What shall we do today?"

Big scary challenges lay ahead, for sure, but I found the unknown exhilarating. As I plopped back into my parents' large sofa and got accustomed to familiar surroundings, I thought back to speaking to one of my best friends at the wedding in Slovenia. He said, "When you come home, it will all be different, but nothing will have changed. You'll be the one that's changed." That throwaway comment had stuck with me and I now understood his perspective: I could think wider now than I ever did before. Anything was possible.

All of a sudden, I got to shape a new life path and curate my ambitions with design, layering it all with this new minimalist mindset I had not only just discovered, but was also speaking directly to me. I was converted – inexplicably out of nowhere, but also not. The very thing I had been searching, grasping for before I left, I found while travelling when my head was clear of clutter. I was no longer existing on my own default setting, reacting after things happened; now I got to be the architect of my own life. And set my own course.

A few days into living with the parents again and we were settling in fine. I'd done some life admin by donating the majority of the hair on my head and face to the local barbershop floor and changing any remaining foreign cash back into pounds.

"Life admin'" is as exciting as it sounds, isn't it? Completing all the boring odd jobs in life that need doing: updating addresses, renewing utilities/subscriptions/insurances, and sorting through bills. For an organised introvert with a thirst for getting the best deal, life admin can be quite an enjoyable task, some of the time.

The first few days in the new normal were slow, steady and restful, but needed, what with the discombobulation of jet lag. We had our own bedroom and en-suite to store all our remaining belongings. The fold-out bed, usually reserved for occasional guests, was comfortable enough for our short-ish stay. Through habit, we were still in the "living out of our bags" headspace; a few of our smarter clothes were hung up on the backs of chairs and door handles, but other than that, most of our clothes were folded and stacked up on the floor. This spare room was bigger than the bedrooms in our old flat, but it contained considerably more stuff.

To the right of the bed was a small oak bookshelf that held old children's books, autobiographies from the 80s and 90s and binders of incomplete subscription magazines containing parts of unfinished models. "Pay 99p for magazine number one with the first five pieces and then £7.99 each month for more magazines containing the remaining two hundred pieces," the covers all seemed to read. Waste of time.

At the back of the room were two large wardrobes that were filled to the brim with my mum's no-longer-worn clothes. On top of the wardrobes sat fat cases containing old cables and wires. The cases were supposed to hold my dad's old drum kit but instead of protecting a snare and toms, they stored hundreds of leads for god-knows-what instruments and accompanying gadgets. Behind the door were a stack of blank CDs and floppy discs that spilled onto a mixing desk and chair.

My old childhood bedroom was across the hall. We used this room as our mini-living space. By the door was a large set of drawers against the wall that included sewing instruments, napkins and clothing accessories. Sitting on top of those drawers were around a dozen knick-knacks and tiny bowls with buttons, batteries and foreign coins. A tiny two-seater sofa was our bit of comfort alongside our small old bedroom TV. The alarm clock TV.

The wardrobe I used during my teens and a second, bigger wardrobe, resided in this room. Again, both were now filled with my mum's clothes. Stuck to the door of my old wardrobe there was still a 'big head' caricature of me from a trip to Vegas in 2003. On top were my old football trophies and a dusty, deflated signed ball from the 1994 Charlton Athletic squad which I won in a raffle. The signatures were well and truly faded away, but I could never read any of them anyway due to the haphazard and rushed scrawl of the players. The windowsill was lined with a scattershot of trinkets, music boxes and small toys that no longer worked. There was one large photo frame which held no picture.

Across the hall, my brother's old bedroom contained a few of our boxes from the flat, kitchenware and books mainly. They were stacked on top of crates of wool and knitting needles. There were two more wardrobes in there as well, full of more of my mum's clothes but also some of my dad's suits, only worn on special occasions. At least he had some space, I laughed. The biggest thing taking up most of the floor space were two broken-down drum kits, one digital, and another standard full size with accompanying stands for cymbals. Walking around these rooms I realised the amount of stuff that was choking up this house, the four-bedroom Georgian detached family home my parents had owned since 1991. Only two permanent residents lived there now but I would guess that they had just as much stuff now as when we all lived there together. It was, and still is, a lovely house. But, living there again as an adult, I couldn't help but not see the forest for all the trees. Decades' worth of stuff were designated pockets of space and left as obstacles in the way to get to and from other things. It was probably something I had noticed in the past when visiting but never actually thought too much about. It was how my parents chose to live. But now, with my minimalist mindset, that clutter was front and centre and quite literally in my face. I was motivated to help my folks get rid of it. All of it.

· · · · · ⊜ · · · · · ·

I officially returned to work in a month's time, following our descent back into London. Luckily, my job was still vacant, so that provided a little bit of financial stability whilst we figured out our endgame and life strategy. It was actually pretty straightforward for Hayley to jump back into her old media company – one email to her former manager asking if there were any vacancies was all it took. Don't ask, don't get, I suppose. Hayley would return after only one week of decompression from travelling and from the North (Midlands) after spending some time seeing her family. Her work did apparently fill the vacancy after she left but just before we returned, someone in the same team had also resigned so the timing was perfect. Hayley is brilliant at co-ordinating all the techy media stuff, so I was not surprised they wanted someone of her calibre back quickly. Funny how things just work out like that. She would be making the simple transition back into her old role officially as a new member of staff, again, but this time, I had a feeling she would forego the painful train, Tube, bus route and take the longer and more relaxed drive instead.

Things for me, however, were completely different. I had started to plot a few new moves during the down time in Vietnam. Four job interviews were lined up with other firms so I could start to move myself away from the regularity and self-created ceiling I got myself in at my workplace where I was still technically an employee. The first of those interviews was only a couple of days away and all my smarter clothes and shoes were in a suitcase which had been placed up the loft in my parents' house.

As a child I was always intrigued by the concept of lofts and the mysterious belongings they held. Lofts, or basements, were generally depicted as being scary in films – *Home Alone*, for example – but potentially they were also full of riches and treasure. When I lived at home as a boy and teenager, and having a slight fear of heights, I used to only climb halfway up the rickety stairs to the upper echelons of the house, fearful that I would fall five-foot to my death. My dad would usually lead the way, being the only person who could truly manipulate the hatch, stairs and light all in one smooth operation. Every single time without fail, he would curse about the volume of stuff up there and how he couldn't find this or that whenever the mood suited him to go searching for it. Which was rare.

"I don't know why she keeps this stuff!" would be a regular complaint of the loft, but also his wife. Dad wasn't completely blameless, of course, and my brother had also just left a heap of his crap here as well since moving into his one-bed place, ten minutes down the road, a couple of years ago.

Mum would often send Dad up there to retrieve something that she needed for that afternoon's baking session or to support some activity. She never went up there herself, of course, and I actually don't think she's ever once scaled those steps. She would, however, project manage his efforts from the landing. He would shout down and report about his failed attempts to retrieve whatever it was she had requested and she would of course guide him, knowing exactly where the thing was and in exactly which carrier bag she would have left it in, irrespective of having never been up there. It was like a weird superpower she had, being able to see things through walls and ceilings, yet the stairs themselves were her kryptonite.

As I climbed the wobbly steps up into the loft to retrieve my suitcase full of work clothes, I entered what appeared to be a large space filled with "just in case" purchases and keepsakes, collections and valuables, this and that, bits and bobs, odds and ends, souvenirs and forget-me-nots. It was all there in this sub-urban Aladdin's cave. It felt like an exclusive museum, where all the antiquities of old were on display to nobody, much like in *The Goonies*. But far shittier. It took a few seconds of scanning around the dim-lit space before I locked eyes onto the suitcase. I clambered over bags of VHS videos – remember them? – and boxes of magazines – remember them? – to grab hold of what I needed, all the while my dad shouting commands from below.

"Watch where you put your feet!"

I pulled the suitcase from its resting place and subsequently shifted bin bags full of pillows and bedding with it before carefully lowering it down the hatch into my dad's hands as he stood at the bottom of the steps.

As I carefully positioned myself to step down onto the ladder, I spotted dozens of old board games, action figures, sticker albums, tons of toys, more drums and instruments. Football memorabilia, curtains, quilts and other soft furnishings were littered amongst garden furniture, hampers and cardboard boxes. In the corner, away from all of the stuff, were hundreds – if not thousands – of Dad's vinyl records neatly lined up in a makeshift wooden case.

"There's a lot of stuff up here!" I yelled down. My interest was suddenly piqued.

"I *know.*"

I reached the bottom of the steps and Dad was quick to start folding up the ladders and close the latch; the speed of this process displayed a level of expertise in handling it all but it was also an attempt to try and forget about the volume of crap up there. Out of sight, out of mind.

I pulled the heavier than anticipated suitcase into our make-shift bedroom and unzipped it to reveal a whole load of clothes I had completely forgotten about. Jumpers, shoes and shirts that had initially got through the first round of decluttering at the flat were neatly folded up and ready to be left, admired and not used. However, this time there would be no compromise.

No more Mr Nice Guy.

A number of shirts got unfolded, inspected, quickly folded back up and put into a pile on the bed. The same process was completed with jumpers, shorts and pairs of shoes. It was a swift and calculated extraction/execution similar no doubt to how they killed Osama bin Laden. The thought process was quicker now, one look and I asked myself the same set of questions:

Does this thing add value, or does it serve a purpose?
How many more of these items have I already got?
When was the last time I wore it?

And, most importantly, *Am I really going to wear it again?*

A few items were placed nicely with the rest of my clothes, but the majority were discarded. Within minutes there were large refuse sacks of garments ready to be offered out to my family before being donated. I walked – OK, threw – the bags downstairs and left them by the front door, ready to be taken to the local charity shop.

I retrieved the suit, shirt and tie I required, dusted them off and checked the pockets. Sometimes when I came home drunk or tired, I often left money in my pockets and then months later found a random tenner in my blazer. No luck this time though. Just old train tickets, a spare button and disintegrated receipts – not the best score.

Another couple of suits hung up in the same bag were retrieved from my brother's old bedroom and I swiftly determined that they would also no longer be required. One of them, a deep purple colour, I decided to put on eBay. I took photographs and added views of different angles alongside a detailed brief.

"What are you doing with all those clothes?" my mum asked as she wandered out the kitchen, apron showing dashes of some creation she was working on. Her brow was a little contorted as she stood in the doorway with a quizzical look on her face.

"I'm getting rid of it all," I replied like a man full of purpose. "I don't need them anymore."

"But why, there's so many nice things here."

'Sit down, Mum. I'll tell you why…'

My Mum listened as I broke down elements of my newly formed less is progress mindset. For me, unused and unloved stuff caused blockages. Material items, clutter, junk, whatever you want to call it, got in the way. At its very base level, clutter takes away people's time and attention through cleaning, organising and generally looking for things. I know most of us would rather be doing something else. The deeper you go into its impacts, the more issues it highlights. I personally know how letting go of my stuff gave me back my time, enthusiasm and energy to seek more design to my life. It gave me back control and the feeling of freedom to make better, more deliberate choices. In order to be more, I needed to own, consume and do less. I was determined to not let inanimate objects, decisions of the past, false stories and an unfulfilling job get in the way. I could no longer be fulfilled if my environment was constantly filled.

· · · · · Ⓢ · · · · ·

A ping on the phone drew my attention to a notification from eBay. I was getting accustomed to the various sounds that referenced different phases of the buying and selling process. I was sure they had been well designed to keep sellers/buyers interacting with the platform but, I must say, I did get a little buzz of excitement every time I heard the "kerching" sound or the uplifting "berr-liinngg" when a new bid or message came through. That particular time, someone had shown an interest in the jazzy purple suit and bid £30 for it. After pondering over the offer for maybe five seconds, I concluded that I was happy to let it go, so I worked out the additional postage and agreed to send it to them as soon as possible. Whilst communicating with the buyer, a mum of two, she explained that her fourteen-year-old son had picked this out and would be delighted that hers was the winning offer. Without any prompt, another long message came through as she provided details about how he really wanted to wear it at some school celebration he had coming up. What a way to reinvent, and recycle, this suit, I thought. An item of clothing that I hadn't worn for more than five years, was now getting a re-launch into the Gen-Z population. Who knew where it would end up?

I imagined the young lad rocking up to his school hall in my old suit, looking fresher than a motherfucker as he threw open the doors and 'All of the Lights' by Kanye West tore up the speakers. In slow-mo, this kid adjusted his shirt collar and all his classmates looked on in awe. Before, he was mocked and bullied for his dress sense, but in that moment, he was *the man*. Although this was all a work of fiction in my own head, that's how I saw this purchase panning out for them. It was nice to give someone else the opportunity to make use of something that would have just sat in a wardrobe, unused and unloved, for probably decades had I not made the decision to give it a new lease of life. Maybe that suit would be a talking point for the rest of his life? Maybe there would be pictures taken in that "legendary" suit that would be put in frames on relative's fireplaces for years to come. If he was feeling confident maybe he'd even wear it to his first job interview? Or wedding? Maybe this suit would transform this lad's life – who knows? I felt so pleased it had gone to a good home: proof that decluttering was not just benefiting me, it was also benefiting the community and... future generations. To me, this wasn't just minimalist behaviour – this was also being a little maximum-ist. I was *maximising* the suit's potential... and it made me feel good.

16. Reframing the Value

The sheer volume of clutter in my parents' loft had started to play on my mind. I was unable to walk past it without re-evaluating its usefulness. Before my interviews, I had the ability to stop and think, to reflect on things, to see alternative paths, to see the box and then think outside of it, to be *intentional*. Travelling had done a number on me, for sure. I was a changing man. Even my parents could see it. "Where's old Chris gone?" my mum would say every time I said something that perhaps the "old me" wouldn't have ever dared said.

Before, the stuff in the loft would have been looked at but not seen. I couldn't unsee the items up there, especially the nostalgic stuff I had more of a connection to, such as the football cards, memorabilia, toys and action figures. Those once-loved items were now stored away but for what purpose and why? I was not sure. But, clearly, I was on a quest to find out.

My mum was the one who had the emotional attachment to many of the belongings up the loft. The toys that had been retained were more than just something we played with, the toys and clothes were her favourite things that reminded her of her two boys when they were boys. Rather than isolating the ray gun for what it was – a colourful piece of plastic that made an irritating noise when you pulled the trigger – my mum saw it as something that united my brother and I, as little kids in play, laughing and running around with it, probably in just our pants in the garden. That particular memory would have likely been super fun at the start, creating a story in the garden with inanimate objects like a rake and empty pots but soon ending in tears as I probably would have thrown the gun at Gary, which would have made him cry. (I'm still convinced he would put on the crocodile tears just to get me into trouble.) Every old toy, or item of clothing, had a loving memory attached to it and those memories were safely stored in the loft, so that my Mum could never forget them, and also re-connect with them if she ever felt the need. Which, of course, she never did. To dispose of them was difficult, they were a safety net in case she forgot the memory. It was the same reason mum would always encourage us to keep hold of stuff or find a place for it. Just in case. I understood that concept, emotionally – and found it sweet, reassuring even, that my mum felt this way. But now all I saw was clutter getting in the way of personal growth. Getting in the way of them doing other things with their time.

"When you have kids, you can pass these toys down to them," she said.

I noticed she said, "When" not "if".

Mum projected this scenario from her own imagination which featured her as Grandma, sitting in the corner of the room watching as Hayley and I demonstrated to our fictitious kids how to play with a headless He-Man and a one-armed Ultimate Warrior. One would have a Lego brick and the other a weapon from a lost Thundercat and they would fight to the death, AKA smashing against each other until one of the kids got bored. The arena would be a discoloured farmyard used to house small army figures that would be sticky underneath but mainly covered with World Cup Italia '90 stickers. As beautiful and scary as that sounded, those toys could represent something else. They could still play their part in our family's reality today, not one that was made up.

It was a fantasy I tried not to indulge. And, besides, I was not convinced any kids would want to play with old toys like this. Aren't they all on iPads and Fortnite?

"Dad, let's get back up there and have a look at those toys," I commanded.

My dad rolled his eyes in the way only dads can.

I led him up the stairs, in an attempt to motivate him to take another crack at the loft. Looking back at him, his reluctance was clear to see. Hunched shoulders, lowered head and a slower climb than normal. He already looked dejected and defeated. I found it funny. It's another chore he had been asked to participate in when all he wanted to do was sit on the sofa and watch the cricket.

"She won't let you get rid of anything," he warned me in an attempt to give up the quest before it had even begun.

I advised him my intention was not to throw anything away willy-nilly, it was merely just to explore and spend some time understanding if any of it was worth anything. In fairness, it was the family's stuff. They were not just mine or my brother's toys, neither were they labelled as my parents' stuff because they were stored in their home and they mostly paid for them back in the day. We were all responsible for this stuff and therefore should all have a say in what was done. However, I felt like I was the only one who could step up and advance this intervention. And, besides, they would all thank me when they had a few extra quid in their pockets and less crap in the loft.

"There could be a goldmine up here and you wouldn't even know it," I proclaimed to Dad as we surveyed the littered loft landscape.

"Fools' gold," he mumbled.

Although it was the middle of the day, the loft was dark with only one dim-lit bulb providing a dull glow. The further away from the stepladder we went, the darker and scarier it got. With each step I was overly cautious to make sure I walked on the wooden beams following the old man's advice from earlier. I was having to stretch and step over bags upon bags of stuff just so I could reach the first row of toys. Those few months of consistent yoga and Pilates while travelling were about to come in handy. I quickly concluded that there was no way I could open up the boxes and look into them, so they had to be taken down into the light to rummage through. I was quite happy to do this as it reduced the risk of me sticking my hand into a bag of stuff that had not been opened for years. It could have liquefied for all I knew. There could be an infestation of creepy crawlies in the dark spots. Urgh! A few years ago, my dad did say that there had been a wasps' nest in the corner of the loft which prevented him coming up here, though they eventually did get someone in to remove it, but that was at the back of my mind.

I began to lower boxes and bin bags down to my dad as he looked up at me from the bottom of the stairs, arms open. That look of annoyance was still visible. He was missing vital overs in the Test match and he wanted me to know it was my fault. The first bin bag was handed down and a white label with writing in a blue felt tip on it fell away, disintegrated. What once would have been an indication of the contents was now illegible. A grey plastic box was handed down next, swiftly followed by some old supermarket carrier bags with rips in. Approximately ten bags and boxes full of stuff was lowered down. My dad's patience hit its limit.

"No more, Chris, that's enough for now," he shouted up.

I manoeuvred myself so I could take a look at the landing and we had covered half the floor, so I agreed. Before I exited the loft, I purposefully looked back at the area I had cleared away and I'd hardly made a dent. It was a reality check and a serious one at that. It was a big job, but a job I was willing to do, if only for the sense of gratification and curiosity itch it would scratch. My hands were black with dust as I patted them down and climbed down the ladder.

I began to see familiar muscular arms and legs of 1980s action figures creeping out of the bags, maybe trying to make a run for it. Sharp plastic parts of who-knows-what pierced the lower section of the split supermarket sacks. The grubby boxes of football magazines left their mark on a freshly hoovered carpet. Before the stuff had even been looked at in detail, it was leaving a stain on everyday life. As my dad closed the loft hatch my mum walked up the stairs and tutted at the mess on the floor. Her immediate reaction was one of anger and my dad's default response was to point the finger at me.

"No, no, no!" Mum growled.

"You can't just go throwing this stuff out, it's important… What is it?"

My dad laughed loudly.

"Toys, videos, I'm not fully sure, Mum, so I'm just going to go through it and that's it," I responded calmly in an attempt to provide some reassurance to her. "I'm not going to just throw it out… I'm going to give it a new, better life."

The three of us stood on the landing looking at these dusty boxes and ripped bags of stuff was quite a scene. My Mum's body language was a mix of complete panic, confusion and intrigue. My Dad, with his hands on his hips, was staring at the stuff as if it was another chore, but also, he seemed interested to know what was in the mystery bags. I surveyed the scene with a huge sense of excitement as I already knew the conclusion. I already could guess the ending. I knew that some of this crap was worth a bit of money and, if not, other families and communities could gain value from it. If I could just show my parents the way, it would hopefully inspire them to take a look at the remainder of the clutter after we were no longer living there. And, who knows – they might enjoy letting more of it go.

I opened one of the boxes and the first item I pulled out was *Dangermouse Saves the World* on video cassette. The case and tape still looked in good condition but whoever watched it last didn't even have the decency to be kind and rewind. Granted it could have been me back in the late 80s but that minor annoyance from my youth came flooding back. How many times did I pick up a VHS to watch but then have to stand and wait an extra ten minutes for the slow VCR to rewind the tape to the beginning? Heathens!

"Do you have a VCR anymore?" I asked my dad.

"This was one of your favourites," he joked, trying to avoid the inevitable. I have a feeling he'll be saying that a lot over the next few hours.

"Somewhere… probably."

I purposefully left a silence to see who out of my parents would come up with the excuse to keep these videos first. No one filled it.

Four *Simpsons* videos were next out the box, again still looking well preserved. These were definitely my brother's.

Two *M.A.S.K.* cartoon tapes were retrieved next, definitely mine. One of the corners of the cases had been chipped but the tapes inside looked decent. Disney films, pirate copies of movies from the 90s and random cartoons such as *The Shoe People*, a village of talking shoes, and *Around the World with Willy Fog*, a feline version of *Around the World in Eighty Days*, sat at the base of the box, unused, waiting to be loved again.

Sparks of emotion spread like wildfire through my body as I stacked the tapes up on the floor, reading the back of each one, testing my knowledge. The 80s theme tune to *M.A.S.K.* rang around my head.

"Masked crusaders, working overtime, fighting crime, FIGHTING CRIME!"

I had a flashback to my flat, on the floor, surrounded by piles of clutter – and the buzz I got from organising it all down to something manageable.

Part of me wanted to leave the mess, grab my phone and watch an episode of *M.A.S.K.* on YouTube but that option would always be there, I could relive it later in the day.

I watched as my mum and dad rummaged through the box and laughed at some of the contents. The process itself was fun. It evoked memories that had been stored away. Not particularly useful memories, but memories, nonetheless.

"Do you want to keep these?" I asked them.

No response.

The three of us spent the next couple of hours looking through decades' worth of stuff, pulling out action figures and magazines, chuckling at the bizarre faces and purchase decisions.

"Oh, Chris, look at this, do you remember…" was said every other minute once something new was discovered. We shared stories whilst sitting on the floor wiping dirt off WWF wrestlers and putting broken contents into separate rubbish bags.

What piqued my parents' intrigue was the online demand for some of the things in the bags. A quick bit of research on eBay and a look at the current landscape of items for sale on collectors' websites and other market platforms, provided us all with considerably more information, and confidence, about how valuable some of this shit – sorry, clutter – was.

A whole new world opened up to both of them. The full picture of why they kept all this stuff was partly sentimental, but they also just didn't know how best to discard the items. These items were put up the loft before sites like eBay and Music Magpie existed. Their options and view of the world at the time was limited, so for them it was a case of either throwing things in the trash or keeping them. Of course, some of the items held far too much emotional and financial value to just simply throw away so there they stayed and gathered dust. Over the years, as the options started to become wider and marketplaces became more accessible, particularly online, the overwhelming volume of the stuff became the blocker. There was no easy place to start, so I guess, they just didn't. Reading between the lines, they just wanted someone to hold their hand through it all. I was happy to oblige. I wanted to do it. I needed to do it. It stoked the flames of inspiration that were growing inside of me – the yearning to live a minimalist experience. And they do say that charity begins at home.

Following some sorting, separating and re-organising, the items that still worked and stood the test of time were stacked up in my old bedroom against the only available wall. A Thundercat's lair with accompanying miniature characters and weapons, figures from the He-Man and Transformers franchises and random bits of Ecto-One from Ghostbusters were all cleaned up and gathered together. Incomplete World Cup and 90s Premier League sticker albums were layered up alongside. Most of the items looked good enough to immediately put on eBay and Gumtree for a few weeks to really find out if any of it was still of value to other people. I spent the next few hours taking pictures on my phone and looking up all the relevant information of these items: the date of manufacture, current market value and any sets or collections they were part of. This took time but is wasn't wasted.

Growing up, I was surrounded by music. Most Saturday nights, up until twelve or thirteen, my brother and I would go to my grandparents' bungalow and they would babysit us whilst my mum and dad's band, Rainbow's End, played in old working men's clubs, social clubs and dinner dances around London. My dad played the drums and my mum was the group's lead singer as they smashed out covers of classic songs. Even when they strolled back into my grandparent's place about 2am to pick us up, they still had to shower before going to bed to get rid of all the cigarette smoke and sweat that had clung to them during the night. My dad's set of drums was still in the loft and still reeked of smoke. My brother picked up the sticks when he was old enough and my obsession with crate digging in record shops and finding new music physical and digital led me to the radio, then to learn to DJ and then subsequently to set up Souterrain. But it was my dad's vinyl collection that really fascinated me when I was younger. He was a collector. To my dad, vinyl was more than just a way to play music – it was music. He loved the way it smelled, felt, looked. It transported him to a magical place inside his own head. He would keep his LPs in a storage unit in the living room, right next to the record player. For hours on end, he would sit on the floor looking through them deciding which one to play next before removing it from the sleeve and carefully placing it on the turntable. I watched him give the needle a blow each time to remove any dust before carefully placing it on the exact track he wanted to hear. It was like a skill that only adults could master. And it was little wonder he kept all of his collection safe. Out of sight, but only just.

Throughout the early 90s, I noticed that the LPs coming into the house were getting less and the new trend was to buy CDs, which were smaller, but with a much clearer sound. While his collection grew larger and more varied, Dad's trips to the loft to store the vinyls became more frequent. Over the next couple of decades as us kids grew up and took over spaces in the house, his record collection would move further and further away into the corners of the least-visited area of the home. Slowly overrun by life and the consumption of a family of four, his hobby would subside and play second fiddle to everything else and there the music would stay, untouched and unused. But still there.

As the years rolled on, Dad's music tastes changed. The way he consumed music was vastly different to his habits of the past. He regularly consumed YouTube and played me songs he thought I might like. He'd hand me his iPad with Spotify playing so I could share in his new discovery. The pride in the record collection was still there but his only interaction with them was through stories and a belief that some of the rare pressings and limited editions were now worth a tidy sum. Every now and then we chatted about some old records and he would say, "I've got that in the loft… must be worth a fortune now!" but he would never find out for sure. It was a truth he had created by watching *Antiques Roadshow* and thinking everything older than fifty years was worth money.

The indecision left the vinyl collection up the loft, frozen in time, out of reach, their legend increasing with each year. With no space in the living areas of the home to display them, each day that ticked past increased the risk of deterioration.

"Do you want to know how much your records are actually worth?" I asked him.

Uncertain, dad felt uncomfortable that new information – the truth – would confirm or destroy the story he had been telling himself for so many years.

"OK, let's get a few out and have a look. How will you do it?"

"Discogs," I responded. "It's an online marketplace to buy and sell records, CDs and tapes. It's a collector's heaven." Still learning the site myself, I gave him about as much information as I had found out.

Back up into the loft we went.

Dad had carefully displayed the LPs on a makeshift wooden board and separated each hundred or so with smaller planks of wood. There was some design to it as the more recent 80s and early 90s records were closer to the hatch and the light. I saw classics that I recognised, *Songs in the Key of Life* by Stevie Wonder, some Hall & Oates, Toto, Chicago, Steely Dan and Go West mixed in with bands and artists I'd never heard of. The further you crawled into the darkness, the older the records got. About half of them had an additional plastic sleeve protecting the actual sleeve and those plastic covers were sticky and had years' worth of cobwebs and dust on them. I dared not touch my face after grabbing them, but my dad clearly took care of these babies. Moving more bags out of the way unveiled hundreds more boxes of seven-inch singles and EPs, some records had no sleeve at all and were heavily damaged and warped. Others still looked pretty fresh, these were the ones he thought would be worth something, if anything. I couldn't see all the way down to the end of the loft, but I guessed there were about three thousand records in total.

Back downstairs, I carefully traversed the steps with stacks of vinyl and piled them up on the table in the living room. Mum wasn't best pleased that we, yet again, had tinkered even more with the layout of the loft that she'd never seen. I booted up my laptop, uncertain of where the afternoon would end up. A few weeks earlier, I was walking barefoot in Vietnamese temples. On that day, I was in my mum and dad's kitchen blowing dust and cobwebs off a Cheech and Chong LP.

The layout of the Discogs website was fairly simple and within a few minutes I worked out how to find out the market value of his vinyl stash. Each LP had a unique identifier, a six -to eight-digit reference made up of letters and numbers created by the record label that linked back to a database of millions of albums and singles. All I needed to do to get to the estimated value was punch that number into the search bar and select the exact version he owned. I then had to select the condition of the record from a drop-down list of 'mint', 'near mint', 'very good', 'good' and 'fair'. None of his records were mint because they had been played at least once, so the ones that still looked well preserved, I selected as 'very good'. Once the database had all the information it needed, it quickly went off to calculate the market value of that record in that condition, displaying details of previous sale prices and current sellers and their prices. I quickly became immersed into the level of data that Discogs held. Before I knew it, I had created this repeated anticipation between us.

As I entered in each new LP identifier into the site's search bar, Dad and I devised this game where he would predict which LPs he thought would be worth something and he'd guess how much. He'd pass me the record, sometimes with a brief story attached as to how he came to know of it, I'd search the code and then reveal the true market value to him. On the odd occasion we would find one that was into double figures, a satisfied nod of the head would confirm he knew all along. There was a real sense of satisfaction in being able to answer some of the questions he had pondered all those years. He now had access to all the details he needed to make a better, well-informed decision about their value. He could decide what to do with all these LPs – keep for sentimental reasons or sell for financial ones – safe in the knowledge that his decisions were based on informed and reliable intelligence.

As the days went by, startling discoveries were beginning to be made. He started to see the value emerge with his own eyes.

My mum was more than shocked. She was gobsmacked. My dad was as proud as a peacock, acting like this was his big plan years ago. Together they absorbed this new information.

"There are people out there that are looking for this stuff, collectors, record store owners and fans," I repeated. "Now you know this, what do you want to do?"

"Yeah, let's put a few items up for sale, shall we... and see what happens!'

· · · · · ⓢ · · · · ·

Six weeks later.

Stacks of vinyl litter the downstairs, underneath tables, on top of drawers, in cupboards, on top of cupboards – everywhere. Upstairs, there's boxes of toys and other childhood gear piling up in every room. Although I sat down with the folks and showed them how to punch the record code into the search bar to get the market value of the item, they were quite happy for me to deal with all the various admin and messaging that came with it. They did however get a kick out of looking at each single or LP and then goading each other to see who had the more valuable one. This was both my mum and dad's life up for auction. Each addition to his online vinyl inventory alongside each new bid on a wrestling figure opened up a new piece of information for all of us. We found out all sorts about the demand, who wanted what and where each item was being sold. There were unsolved mysteries within those collections, especially around how he got his hands on versions of records originally released for the Dutch market or where he picked up promo-only copies; Dad didn't know the background to every single one but we all found it fun having a guess.

I was on a bit of a roll with the toys too. I'd offloaded a whole box of He-Man figures for £25 and strangely the incomplete sticker albums were highly contested. There was even a bidding war. My dad had been up and down the road to the Post Office a few times a week; I was sure he was now on first-name terms with the shop assistants.

The old tat that was pushed to the furthest corners of the loft, gathering dust, unloved and unused, topped a grand in the first two dozen sales. It turned out the old soul records that my dad purchased for six shillings and eight pence, small denominations that were no longer used, were highly sought after. His music collection from his youth was now funding his future. And we were all living in this collective minimalist mindset and realising together how valuable it was. Plus, we were spending lovely time together as a family, bonding over a shared experience. All because of an itch I scratched a year earlier.

Motown singles from the 60s, and soul LPs on iconic but long defunct record labels, were fetching hundreds of pounds. This was a shock to all of us. My old VHS cartoons gathered some interest from a teacher at a special-needs school. He messaged me to ask how much I wanted for all of them as I'd put some into different job lots. In the end he just paid for the postage and I donated all of them to that school. That felt good.

Once again, another example that decluttering is not just about making space, earning an extra few quid or taking a load of stuff to the dump, it's also about identifying how your stuff can help others. Even a handful of items can potentially add considerable value to others, but most of us don't know it yet.

A couple of wrestling action figures had gone over the £100 mark after an eBay bidding war between four buyers commenced late into the evening. All the time this was happening live, I was reading the usernames and the bid out to my mum in the style of a horse-race commentator. She was stunned at the price those silly toys she bought in 1990 were going for.

After a busy month of selling, things eventually slowed down, which pleased Hayley as her patience for my decluttering was starting to wane. She was all up for letting go of things not being used but was not a fan of the stuff being stacked up waiting to be sold on. I was deeper into the knowledge and value of decluttering and minimalism. Hayley was happy to take part every now and then but remained a tourist.

Items that had been on eBay for a number of weeks with no interest, I took down and looked to donate or recycle/repurpose instead. Scrolling back through the app, I calculated around 117 sales of just the toys, books, videos, games, magazines, clothes and action figures from the loft totalled £1,340. That money was set aside to go towards a new car. Or a new sofa. Or something else that would enhance or add value to our new living space.

My mum and dad hadn't treated themselves to a proper holiday for about fifteen years. Although at retirement age, they still worked part-time selling plants and flowers down the local market.

My dad did a lot of the heavy lifting whilst Mum, thankfully, was the face of the operation, often helping customers with potting advice. They both worked hard and had done so for most of their lives, so holidays were just forgotten about or too expensive. They needed to keep everything ticking over at home and work was far more important than taking a break. With the sale of a few old records that were stuck up in the loft, festering in the dark, that option to go away for a couple of weeks was now a real possibility and it was not long before I heard them talking about taking a few days off to go to Devon. It wasn't a faraway, exotic destination but it was a start. Not only did they have that opportunity, as well as the tools and knowledge to continue selling old items at their own leisure, but they also had the experiences about this whole period that they could now tell their friends about. Who knows, maybe that would inspire them to clear the rest of the clutter in their loft and their lives. Maybe I started a mini-revolution?

17. Pivotal Failure

"It was just a matter of time!" a colleague exclaimed as they slumped back in their ergonomically enhanced chair.

My resignation came as no surprise. My team all peered over their monitors to look at me as the obligatory "I'm leaving" email popped up in their inbox confirming their suspicions: my time at the company was at an end.

Within two months of connecting the dots in Vietnam and discovering the lifestyle term 'minimalism', I had quit my job for good. I had entirely removed all safety nets. No longer would I be trapped by my previous life choices and the false stories I had told myself for so long. It was time to design a life for myself that allowed me to feel content and contribute. That moment, sat at my old desk, at my old company, in my old suit, in my old life, was the time to break my personal building blocks and rebuild them with new infrastructure, new intention, so I could do more of what I wanted and be the best version of myself. Ten years I'd been there, give or take. Only a three-month notice period kept me from taking my first step onto a new path after accepting an offer from a large financial organisation. I knew most people in the industry I was leaving and had built up my reputation throughout that time, one that I was proud of. Catching bad guys (without having to get up from my chair) was my jam. For the most part, I was comfortably content. I knew everyone, I had good knowledge, the culture at work was decent, I could be fine just plodding along but fine was no longer good enough. I was quickly becoming the guy receiving an award for longevity rather than achievement. I always found them an interesting accomplishment, well done for sticking it out for so long, here's a balloon. It rewarded loyalty to a certain extent, but I was sure the majority of those people had been moaning, kicking off and bad-mouthing the company down the years. You could get acknowledgement for half-assing it for so long. Maybe I should have given more recognition to the pairs of socks and underwear I'd had for the same period of time. The ten-year award was coming up and I was well aware of it. I stayed in my lane and for the longest time that was OK for me. I knew I could offer more, some years I did, some years not so much, but I didn't really know how to articulate my skills and how much value I could add. Underneath the daily grind was a heap of potential and aspirations that were tamed and the longer I stayed around the same place, the more that energy started to dissipate. Taking that time out to open my eyes to the art of the possible brushed off all the rust and elevated me to a higher level of awareness of what I could offer to not just myself, and others, but to life itself.

I always had this assumption or belief that a job was always just a means to an end. To make money for retirement. You did the work so you could afford to live. Maybe I was influenced by the people around me, seeing my parents do pretty much the same thing for decades, or maybe it was me just having a bit of a fixed mindset, but work was something you tolerated and moaned about, but you took it on the chin because it rewarded you financially. "It paid the bills" was a phrase I heard myself saying constantly. On the face of it, my job sounded exciting, maybe it was the way I sold it, maybe it was exactly what I wanted from others, that envy from people to say, "Wow, you must be so talented to be able to catch bad guys." After a while it became a lie; I was bored, felt wasted, undervalued, underpaid and I could see my days drifting away – but I accepted it and just played the victim. Everything was someone else's fault and the reason why people couldn't see my talent was because they were all blind to it. Of course, the truth was, I had become a hostage to my own self-depreciation and limiting thoughts. I was a captive in the self-made prison of my physical, mental and emotional clutter.

There was nothing inherently wrong with being comfortable with your lot, I admire those people who rely on stability to provide for others, but I wanted, needed, something different. I yearned to find more fulfilment in my career. I wanted more control and more flexibility. Whatever the next thing was going to be, it had to align with how I wanted to live my life rather than fill the time. We – all of us – spend a lot of time doing "work", being at "work", going to "work", and whilst I was curating my life of less, I needed something that connected with that. No longer was I happy just being comfortable, I wanted more meaning out of my career and nothing was going to stop me from getting it. If I had to burn down everything I had built up to get there, then so be it.

But this heightened awareness and desire for meaningful, purposeful work still didn't make me immune to the odd fuck-up. What I didn't realise was that there was one more substantial failure around the corner.

As my self-awareness and confidence continued to build, I quickly realised that I would need to remove myself from yet another situation that I had found myself in.

Although I had done the brave but necessary thing of walking away from a stable, comfortable job, I actually ended up falling into the trap I was trying to avoid. Doing the same job for more money, on a bigger scale just in a different company. I was so transfixed on the idea that putting myself in a different environment would give me the kickstart I needed to find fulfilling work, that I lapsed back into the routine of doing the same job, but different. Or "same same, but different!" as all the market sellers in Asia would shout at us when we walked past. Within a few weeks of starting my new and exciting job, I quickly realised I'd made a massive error. It was almost as if I was still so high from being in this 'woke' state and achieving significant things like travelling, leaving my old job and being debt free that I had been distracted from all the new shiny elements in my life, but I still hadn't found what I was looking for, to quote U2. I was my own caricature happily strolling down the road, whistling, content, confident but not looking where I was going and then comically falling down the same fucking manhole I fell into ten years prior.

On February 20, 2018, I interviewed for a job with a large corporation. A week later I was offered and subsequently accepted that job. I worked my way through my three-month notice period and started my new role, once again catching bad guys from behind a desk.

It took me a few weeks in that new job to realise I'd fucked up and then a further nine months to do the thing that I was supposed to have done all along.

I'd gone from knowing everything and everyone to nothing and nobody, but that was part of the plan, that bit was OK. All the excitement of starting something from scratch and being the new guy was washed away within days. I reached another level of awareness that this path wasn't for me and I had to get out, sharpish.

My job title was excessively long and boring, with labels such as 'senior' and 'specialist' which gave off delusions of grandeur that I was an expert in this one area of crime intelligence; it was just all too cringy and false. I hated telling people who asked so I would underplay it.

My first day was a complete mess. I had stacks of information thrown at me and I could quickly see that the team had not recruited a new person from outside their organisation for some years. In the first week I was taken to a meeting and for two hours sat there, silent, as acronyms and corporate waffle were exchanged between a host of middle-aged white men wearing expensive suits whilst drinking expensive coffee. The topic of the day was the intricacies of a process or a system I had no interest in. Nothing changed at the end of the meeting. A lot of words spoken but nothing said. The only thing that left any sort of mark were the coffee-stained rings on the table. It was excruciatingly boring, and not only did I not fully understand what was happening, I also realised that I just simply did not give a shit. Not one.

The weeks that followed were sprinkled with these types of meetings and it became a bit of a running joke with Hayley and me. We would check in with each other via text each day when we were both at work and she would try to guess how many hours I had wasted in pointless meetings; invariably she would guess two to three hours a day and would be right most of the time. I managed to perfect the art of looking interested (boondoggling levelled up then) on the outside whilst mentally wandering off into a happier place. A place where I could add value to people's lives daily, where I could create something that contributed to people's success. A place where my time and skills wouldn't be wasted faking enthusiasm, only creating it.

Everything seemed slow and cumbersome. The processes were over-complicated, sluggish and out of date. The people were tired and worn down. What should have been a bustling area of intelligent, passionate people working on making the organisation and society safer from being entangled in the world of organised crime was actually like a morgue. People were so worried about making a mistake that no one really knew what everyone else was doing, even though they were sitting six feet away. No one tried anything new for fear of getting it wrong or pissing someone else off. One colleague, who was very friendly and made me feel welcome, would come over to my desk most days for a chat. She would end up looking over her shoulder and around the floor whilst whispering. When I asked her why she did that, she said "You never know who is listening."

When I eventually did get around to doing some work, it wasn't clear why I was doing it or who I was doing it for. It was hard for me to understand the value of what I was doing and where it made a difference. More red flags started to appear when I found that the tasks I was spending considerable amounts of time on "may come in handy one day" and would be valuable "just in case something like this happened again". So, basically, my work was to never be seen again, no matter how good, or bad, it was. Where was my incentive? Understanding the danger of those once innocent phrases was clear to me and I'd started to reject them as useful. Those phrases kept me tethered to the past and I could see their impact on the team already. They once again became obstacles between me and progress.

It was only a matter of time before I became disillusioned with the job, so to seek solace I opened up a blank document on my computer and started to keep some notes. What began as a place to track details of who did what, acronyms and 'how to' guides on my new role, quickly became a makeshift journal, a safe space to collect my thoughts and capture what was going on for me in reaction to events occurring within this new workplace. It was my non-judgemental sanctuary away from the deafening silence of the office.

As each week went by, the makeshift journal at work started to reveal a whole heap of information. Patterns and trends of what motivated me and what didn't started to become exposed. Although I was sitting at my desk most days, I realised I needed various outlets to feel engaged and the lack of those outlets set off alarm bells. The journal was holding up the mirror and pointing me towards something like a new set of values, of which two were:

1) Adventure – the ability to try new things and take risks.
2) Influence – having a positive effect on people or things.

More would come but once these values started to formulate, and I had literally written them out, I had to make a choice. Stick with the job, react to this default setting I'd found myself in again and see what happened, running the risk of these values potentially being compromised, or walk away and start again. The journal was clear. My words were clear. It spat out more bad days than good, more negative thoughts than positive. I could feel myself stepping further and further away from the team. Something didn't feel right, and I had to decide whether I would ignore the red flags and wait until I felt OK or do something about it.

The pivotal moment came when I was offered the opportunity to take part in a year-long qualification, costing thousands of pounds but all paid for by the company. This was an additional part of the journey you were encouraged to take, everyone else in the team had already done it. No one had ever turned down this offer before, but I knew if I committed myself to getting pointless letters after my name, I'd be stuck here, years lost again to my own crap decision making. After a few minutes discussing it all over with Hayley, I decided that I would politely reject the offer, and send a clear message to them (and myself) that I was not there for the long haul. It was a shock to my new boss, but it was a simple decision for me. I was grateful for the offer, but I knew that the consequences of saying yes to that would be incredibly damaging to my minimalist mindset and my goal to only bring in what added value. Saying no to this course would mean I'd be able to say yes to other, hopefully more interesting things in the unwritten future. My behaviour may have seemed strange to some, but I knew then, as I know now, that a life by someone else's design is no life at all.

I'd made a mistake taking this job. I had to embrace this failure in judgement. Days were spent in self-flagellation, blaming myself that I had taken the wrong path because I didn't fully know where the right one was. I had to keep searching. I had to rectify the mistake.

On February 20, 2019, a year later, I resigned. Again.

Following my music passion with Souterrain and trying to turn that into some sort of a career had led me down a rabbit hole. Never had I imagined that I would lose that feeling of wonder and enjoyment of just being able to listen to a song. The magic had gone from that experience and I had driven it away by prioritising the time listening to stuff that I found less favourable. Gone was the ability to absorb and be present with my favourite music, instead I was consumed by the quantity and the need for finding the next breakthrough artist before anyone else.

Everything started to sound the same and the moment that listening to a new song and working with an artist became a business option was when it all felt wrong. Following my passion was a wrong turn and it would take me a while to enjoy a new album for what it was without wondering how I could work with the artist in some way.

Putting music aside for a bit meant that I could explore some other things to listen to whilst on regular walks alone, either during my lunch breaks at work, my favourite time of day when I got to walk around the city, or at the weekends, strolling around the green spaces near my parent's house. Clearing my head became associated with clearing my life.

I started to open up to the world of podcasts.

Having spent very little time in this arena I was initially unsure where to begin or what value it would add, but I understood now that disrupting, or letting go of, my traditional thoughts and actions away from what I already knew about careers would require a completely different approach. I needed to declutter what I already knew and start again. I mindlessly started typing search terms into Spotify to see what jumped out. I started a number of popular business, personal development and career boosting podcasts but they were rarely finished. Interestingly, though, the same few names kept coming up in conversation on those podcasts, names I'd never heard of. Author and motivational speaker Simon Sinek was one, author and entrepreneur Seth Godin was another; leadership researcher Liz Wiseman, executive coach and leadership author Michael Bungay Stainier, mindset psychologist Carol Dweck and leading thinker on corporate disruption Whitney Johnson all piqued my interest. I looked for offerings from these people with no expectation other than to explore what was there. Combining those learnings alongside going deeper with absorbing words from Joshua Fields Millburn, Ryan Nicodemus, Cait Flanders, Joshua Becker, Courtney Carver, Leo Babauta and other prominent voices in the minimalist community allowed me to further my proficiency in crafting my own version of what minimalism, simpler living and a fulfilling pursuit meant to me. The time spent putting these learning blocks together allowed connections to start to open up and I found that I was building up a list of "thought leaders" to follow. In this huge warehouse of darkness, I had switched the light on and found a whole bunch of other rooms to walk around in.

I allowed myself to become a sponge and without the physical and mental clutter around me, I could focus on collecting new knowledge instead. I had fears and self-doubt about not understanding some of it or maybe even disagreeing with parts, but I figured that was OK, I didn't need to aim for perfection anymore. I was curious. I was in control and I was gifted with discovering a few more values to add to my new and improved To-Do list, or To-Be list, as I call it today:

3) Freedom – flexibility and agility to move around and using my own initiative and experience to make things better,
4) Creative contribution – the ability to create and design valuable products and offerings. And, finally,
5) Meaningful work – my job contributing to the improvement of society and people.

One of the biggest things I learnt during this period of curious uncertainty – chasing the unknown, as I called it – was the pleasures of a simple walk. A walk can be a life lesson. I went out and I deliberately got lost whilst listening to someone smarter than me on a podcast talk about things that would grow my knowledge and awareness. I slowed down. I took my time. I rambled. I meandered. I let my legs take me for as long as they'd let me. I was listening to interviews and discussions about leadership skills, coaching, workplace cultures, talent development, human behaviours, mindsets, purpose and motivation. Each thought leader I listened to opened my mind to different ways of living, working, approaching challenges, dealing with mistakes and thinking way outside the box. It made me question everything. The first podcast I stumbled on was *Career Relaunch* by Joseph Liu as I was looking to pick up hints on how to craft myself away from this latest shit job into something more meaningful. I then quickly moved on to *How to be Awesome at Your Job* hosted by Pete Mockaitis, which had an incredible back catalogue of shows I could dive into. I found great solace in shows that shared stories rather than a preachy list of things that I should be doing to be successful. In fact, here's a playlist of podcasts that I found valuable during that time (and still listen to now):

1. *Good Life Project* by Jonathan Fields
   Inspirational conversations about living a fully engaged life.
2. *Disrupt Yourself* by Whitney Johnson
   Expertise in disruptive innovation and personal disruption
3. *Talent Development Hot Seat* by Andy Storch
   Dedicated to developing people.
4. *The Minimalists Podcast* by Joshua Fields Millburn & Ryan Nicodemus
   Discussing living a meaningful life with less.
5. *How to be Awesome at Your Job* by Pete Mockaitis
   Stories and advice on, well, how to be awesome at your job
6. *Optimal Living Daily: Personal Development & Minimalism* by Justin Malik
   Reading the best content on personal development, minimalism, productivity and more (you'll find some of my articles on here too.)
7. *The Art of Decluttering* by Amy Revell & Kirsty Farrugia
   Professional Organisers helping their clients declutter.
8. *Akimbo* by Seth Godin
   A podcast about culture and how we can change it.

I was also recommended a few from people in my circle, so a special mention to Garry Turner's *Value Through Vulnerability* podcast, which I was fortunate enough to feature on, and Jeff Weigh's *Perfect Imbalance* show, which I was also on. Since then, I've set up a podcast with two other coaches called *Goodism* which would be another treat for your ears. I could go on, but that's probably enough. We don't need excess lists in a book about less.

That previous dark warehouse now had all the lights turned on and in the centre was a massive ball pit, which I dived into head-first and swam around in. The podcasts continued to support the learning structure I had accidentally found myself in, which then led to exploring and compiling more knowledge online. I went down numerous rabbit holes of information and stumbled upon a number of free webinars to join. Some were good, some were meh, but the information collection continued apace. I was learning, absorbing, gleaning the good bits and abandoning the bad. I formed opinions and I stood on the shoulders of others, quoting them to myself. The online freebies then turned into courses that I actually wanted to join, and I started delving into Open University courses on empowerment, coaching, teamwork, motivation, emotional intelligence. I was learning how to learn again. I was learning how to listen. I never knew that listening was so hard. I mean, really listening, focusing and concentrating hard on every word that someone was saying, how they were saying it and being attentive. Being with them intentionally. Most of us, I'm sure, are OK listeners but generally just waiting for our turn to speak or already formulating a response. I learnt how to hear what someone was saying and, sometimes more importantly, what they weren't. Try it.

Some days at work, I took myself off to courses ran by external speakers on various topics like leadership and productivity. Sometimes I just woke up and disappeared in my head for hours or networked with people who had any element of coaching in their job title. I started to spit out theories and facts during conversations that cemented their place in my brain somehow, throwing out stats such as, "It can take a minimum of sixty-six days to build up a new habit to feel automatic." I started to formulate my own and used them in conversation. "Multi-tasking is a risk, not a skill" was one that I've heard quoted back to me. Even if someone disagreed, it was a conversation starter, and I was instigating new ways of thinking.

I surrounded myself with a whole new diverse group of interesting thought leaders and curious minds. My LinkedIn connections became full of people who I actually wanted to engage with and discuss ideas with rather than just celebrate the odd work anniversary.

This period was my learning curve. I threw out the old and filled in the blanks with new information. I was learning new things, not because a job required me to, but because I found personal value in it. It made me better and it was making the people around me better by becoming more aware of the things they did and the potential they had. Hayley would often comment that I was spending more time watching Ted talks than football. I enjoyed the path I was on, regardless of not really knowing where it was leading me. I was enjoying the journey.

I locked into more individuals like Dr Andy Cope (official Dr of Happiness – I've read his book *Be Brilliant Everyday* three times, it's great, he's great.) and elite performance coach Jamil Qureshi (incredible at what he does and could also be a top stand-up comedian – he cracked a great joke once at a talk I went to at work, I was the only one who laughed out loud in a room full of stiffs) who seemed like they were doing something that sounded as if it aligned with what I was looking for: ideas that inspired, provoked, created, taught. Ideas that unlocked people from their daily drudgery. That helped them be better. Inspiration for the uninspired. I gravitated towards any person who was filling the world with ideas that sparked imagination, and ideas far outside the realm of just minimalism. Anything to do with mindfulness, human talent, behaviour and coaching, I would read what they wrote and listen to them speak, and it would give me questions to ask myself and others such as, "What challenges have I overcome?" and "What do I define as success?" My view of the world got even broader and I got through the days of uncertainty by completing the work tasks I had to do as quickly as possible so I could spend more time sharing my learning and challenging traditional processes with colleagues who were interested.

After a few weeks of chasing my curiosity and spending hours down fascinating information-gathering rabbit holes, I had my next eureka moment.

I was on a train back to my parents' house from work, standing next to a bunch of strangers as it rattled slowly from London Bridge. I found that my most enjoyable moments at work in the past and recent present had been when I was supporting others. When I was helping, mentoring, coaching and leading. When I was being that trusted person for someone to just talk out their blockers. I had naturally progressed over the years from being more technically focused to finding more value in being more people focused. That's what energised me and, similar to decluttering, but not knowing about the minimalism label, I was coaching, kind of, but without an awareness of what coaching was or indeed whether it was an actual job. That itch of having more to offer was starting to be scratched, I wanted to set my sights on becoming a better coach and supporting more talented people to really unlock their potential. That was a lightbulb moment for me – *I wanted to help others learn what I had learnt.*

I could feel the value of speaking to people and doing new things but there was no immediate magic button that turned a shit job into a good one, however I could sense that I was heading in the right direction. Focusing positively on aligning my values to my purpose of coaching others helped me keep motivated whilst doing stuff I didn't want to do. Within a few months of speaking to people around the organisation, a new role all of a sudden came into view. Through a maze and myriad of colleagues pointing me in this direction and that direction, telling me to speak to this person and that person, eventually I did find the right person and not one, not two but three vacancies presented themselves to me. Three! Three attempts to walk away from the mistake and a job that didn't fit. Although an interesting turn of events, I saw it as a reward for being proactive and throwing metaphorical magnets out everywhere attracting back more of what I'd put out.

You'll be pleased to know that on the third attempt I landed the coaching job. I didn't even get an interview for the first two, and that was because I hadn't put a couple of buzzwords in my

CV, but I added them in the third time. Once I got the offer, I felt like I'd finally arrived at where I wanted to be. The first green light on a new journey. I now knew what my values were and now I had a job that aligned with those. It took discipline but my mindset of living a meaningful life got me there. I wasn't going to passively drift like I had done before, I was designing my life and the career would play a huge part in that.

A few months after walking away from one career and starting another, I started to get messages from old colleagues who relayed to me that seeing me leave after less than a year sparked a series of events where 50 per cent of the team I had got to know had since moved on into new, more fulfilling jobs, some into new companies completely. They said that seeing me not settle for something that didn't motivate me shocked them into action. They saw me redesign what a meaningful career meant and wanted the same for themselves. By me disrupting myself, I accidently ended up as this beacon that others could copy or look to. Even my boss, who interviewed me for the role, dropped me a text six months later simply saying "I've resigned".

Looking back on it now, I bet that department weren't best pleased with my disruption, but I doubt they would have even known I was there. By embracing this awkward but pivotal failure, I came to view bumps in the road not as a problem but as an opportunity to adapt and learn.

Of course, 2020-21 will likely go down in history as the longest bump in the road for most, but some of us, myself included, found opportunity in the chaos. Failing wasn't deemed as successful before, but for me it was now a First Attempt In Learning (F.A.I.L).

18. Digital Declutter

After a few too many months living with my parents, Hayley and I moved into our new flat, still in south-east London but a part of the capital that was walking distance to a huge park. We could jump on a train around the corner and be into London Bridge or Victoria within twenty minutes and also stroll down the road to be close to trees and nature. The two-bed, two-bath flat was plenty for us because we had significantly less stuff than we ever did. Each room got used to its full potential, we didn't need any more space than that.

All my clothes fitted nicely into one wardrobe and there was no organised disarray. Minimalism was having a positive, and persistent, impact on me. However, it hadn't really occurred to me too much about the clutter I had in my digital life. Because there was not a physical thing getting in the way, or something that I could touch or see, the volume of stuff on my phone and laptop didn't really register as excess. But my digital life was just as cluttered as my physical one used to be. My social media was packed full of crap accounts that I no had longer any interest in. My Twitter timeline had become littered with more negative opinions and everything seemed to be an outrage between the left and the right. I had 'friends' on Facebook that I'd never spoken to or engaged with meaningfully in any way. Some of them would just use the platform to moan about some meaningless tosh or spout a load of vile shit. My LinkedIn account was a scattered and disorganised web of worthless connections, I had no idea who some of them were plus a considerable amount were a window into a past that I was quickly moving away from. Although I read some experiments about just deleting those platforms altogether, personally I still gained some value from them. My version of a minimalist lifestyle was not to starve myself of technology but to make it work better for me. Streamline. Facebook was a decent tool to stay in contact with distant relatives but without some curation it was quickly becoming a place that just reminded me of people's birthdays. I enjoyed a lot of football opinions and articles on Twitter but there was also a lot of shit that I had followed down the years, like the latest alien invasion conspiracy theorists, so like everything else I had done, I removed what didn't add value and amplify what did. I deleted people I didn't need and added those I felt I did. I needed to re-design how social media and my digital life in general would serve me.

If I was going to gain value from using social media, rather than pointless scrolling, I needed to constantly re-evaluate what I allowed to steal away my time and attention. I needed to curate them now and keep monitoring them moving forward, otherwise I'd just slip backwards into bad habits. You could say I conducted a digital MOT, always asking whether the tech in my hands enhances or consumes my life.

Other than taking some simple steps to get really intimate with the ignore and unfollow buttons, one of my key successes was with LinkedIn. If I was going to continue to learn and connect with thought leaders across the world, this would be a great place to do that, however my profile at the time didn't say anything. I had over 650 connections, the majority of which were people that I had maybe worked with way back or spoken to once in the past. Some I couldn't tell you how or why we were connected. They certainly weren't getting any value from me; I hadn't posted anything for years. It would need a full-on *Unsolved Mysteries* episode to get to the bottom of it. It was full of crap that needed decluttering, so I spent a few hours one afternoon ditching over 400 connections. I then redesigned my profile, removed any technical jargon that no one outside my old industry would know, updated my achievements and aspirations and followed some of the influential people who I had spent time listening to via their podcasts. Over time a new, highly engaging network of diverse connections started to form. I connected with people who I aspired to be like, who had great opinions and different ways of viewing the world. It was no longer going to be a glimpse back into a past that I couldn't learn from, it would be a useful tool to help me in the present and show me potential pathways in the future.

Personally, if you're going to use LinkedIn, identify what person you want to be and surround yourself with those types of people. Even your current job title could be holding you back, tethered to a label you want to relinquish. The dangers of staying linked to past roles, people and industries is that it becomes all you see, so you could struggle to think wider than what you already know. And when it comes to changing your career and looking for more fulfilling work, thinking wider is one of the greatest skills you can learn.

I also had several email accounts that required maintenance. An unused Hotmail account I had maybe for more than a decade that was gathering mostly spam. One connected with Souterrain, another personal Gmail account, the travel Gmail account that Hayley set-up, plus an old inbox that was given to me when I first joined Croydon Radio back in 2012. Five email accounts. I had been blind to this for ages but now, after months of learning and listening to minimalist experts and reading *Digital Minimalism* by Cal Newport, I knew that digital decluttering helped free up storage of time, attention, the mind, as well as my devices. I just had to tweak the approach to make it work for me.

To be honest, I had no idea of the volume of emails within these mailboxes, so I immediately took the decision to just delete the radio and Souterrain accounts wholesale, like a cold calculated villain, no emotion. Who knew what was in there, but we'll never know and I was OK with that. If it was important, I was contactable on other platforms. It removed the what-ifs and saved me time looking through them all.

My main focus was on the old Hotmail account, my default email for many years. That account was everywhere. I used it to set up all my social media a few years ago, it was on my CV. Everything I had bought online since 2010 had that email attached to it.

Deleting junk or marketing emails on my phone was no trouble. I was into the habit of deleting and swiping them away as soon as they came in rather than just unsubscribing. All that was doing though was just moving one piece of junk from one space to another: moving one email from my inbox to my deleted folder. It was like moving a 'just in case' physical item from the living room into the back of a cupboard. It was out of the way but still taking up space. I had switched off any auto-deletion or archiving rule on my phone. Because, well, you probably already know why.

Deleting these unwanted emails gave me a false sense of control. Yes, there was a sense of satisfaction being able to easily remove stuff, but every day it would come back. That promotion or offer would find its way right back onto my device and steal away my focus and attention. The trade-off didn't seem right, it felt so easy. I allowed numerous companies to show me what they wanted me to buy next and I batted it away multiple times a day, every day.

I started to daydream.

I pictured a vision of me driving, I don't know where I was or what car I was driving but the road was straight. There's greenery on either side of the road, trees maybe, but I couldn't be sure. Cars, bikes and people were everywhere, in front, behind, overtaking. Have you ever tried to cross a road in Hanoi? Like that. I switched from first-person to third-person view and saw loads of brand names sitting in the back of the car. They were all climbing over each other and jostling for position. Some were wearing seatbelts and others weren't.

"WHAT ABOUT NOW?"

I heard this repeated over and over and over again at different volumes, in different accents with different tones.

"WHAT ABOUT NOW, WHAT ABOUT NOW, WHAT ABOUT NOW?"

I did my best to ignore them by turning the radio up and opening the window. It's just noise, all the companies were shouting the same thing at me, it was just waves and waves of noise. Eventually I succumbed to their incessant tone and turned around and shouted.

"SHUT THE FUCK UP!"

Quiet for a moment, the brand names froze and retreated into their seats as I turned back around, eyes on the road, satisfied with my over-the-top response. I let out a deep sigh and regained control of my breath. The road was clearer, I acknowledged the huge trees on either side, they were always there, but I'd never been able to see them. They looked healthy and the birds were happy to sit on the branches and chat away. There was no traffic now. The beats playing through the radio were familiar and I tapped along on the steering wheel as if imagining I was in the band. I saw another car in the distance, I recognised it but paid no attention. The song was nearly finished. Another car drove past me, then another and then another. Traffic was starting to build up again. The birds had gone, the trees had less leaves now. A couple of minutes of calm went by like a flash and I started to hear murmuring behind me again. The companies were gathering up the courage to ask the question again, shuffling and nudging each other trying to goad their competitors into being the first to ask the same question.

"What about now? What about now? What about now? WHAT ABOUT NOW? WHAT ABOUT NOW?"

I turned around to grab hold of the company names in a rage, letting go of the steering wheel. The car started to veer uncontrollably into the middle of the road and before I knew it, everything goes black and I've crashed. There my daydream ends.

I fired up my new laptop, after finally ditching the old one, and logged in to my Hotmail account: 12,316 emails were presented to me. The number bold in the top right-hand corner of the screen. Dozens of back pages of emails were on offer as I started to scroll backwards to the earliest message still sitting in my inbox. The older pages represented my digital loft. Further and further I went back, clicking on the touchpad quicker than the page could load up, impatiently wanting to see the end of my virtual letter box tunnel. Or maybe it was the start?

Eventually I got there, a hundred-odd pages later and I found the oldest piece of digital crap I'd subconsciously been hoarding all these years. April 10, 2012 was the date on the email and it was from a customer service department for a bank that I no longer had any affiliation with. I opened it up. The content was dull. A reminder of my overdraft rates and a promotion on a new credit card offer.

Well done on going overdrawn. Based on your past performance, you look like someone who would also be good at collecting some more debt. Fancy it?

Clearly, that's not exactly what it said, but that's how I read it. At some point in time I had seen this email or at least scanned it for its contents and then decided to keep it. I guess that, at the time, I thought that I would have needed to revisit it one day, but now I know that was never the case. I didn't need it then and, years later, I still don't need it. I was happy to let go of it. Delete.

I quickly sorted the thousands of emails into alphabetical order by sender and that highlighted the volume of rubbish from the same source. That way I could then highlight a whole bunch of emails in one go from one sender and mass delete (and then delete the deleted of course!).

I adjusted the filter to show the list backwards in an attempt to make the task a little more interesting. Starting from Z and gaining some momentum would likely keep me going to battle through the whole lot in one sitting. It was a new tactic I'd learnt recently from James Clear and his *Atomic Habits* book to recognise the small wins so you could prove to yourself you could reach the bigger goal. I was more aware of stepping back and stopping to celebrate the tiny victories and being more aware of the steps and journey to achieve something rather than the longer goal itself.

Dozens of Uber receipts, fast fashion offers, pension details from years ago, documents from expired insurers, attached confirmation of hotel stays, parcel deliveries, dinner reservations and concert tickets all littered my screen. Notifications from social media messages intertwined with weekly guides, magazines, bitcoin spam, job search results and promotions for bars I'd not been to in years. Bank offers, LinkedIn invites, property search results, were all there inviting me to do something uninteresting, unimportant or underwhelming. Messages about irrelevant things from unknown people clogged my digital space. Utilities updates, Converse (of course), eBay, Urban Outfitters, mud runs, National Lottery, calendar notifications, money-saving tips, flight comparison sites. It was a boring but necessary way of holding the mirror up to my spending habits and interests down the years. There was junk everywhere. Articles and blogs I'd signed up for but never read. Updates I highlighted and saved but never got back to. Jobs that I showed a slight bit of interest in but never applied for.

I found seven emails that were worth keeping, temporarily. Seven out of 12,000. None of them were over two weeks old.

Once the senders were all bunched up together, I opened one for each of them and purposefully clicked 'unsubscribe'. I made sure I unticked all relevant boxes and followed any instructions provided so that I knew I should never get another email from them again. I wanted to see it for my own eyes.

Then, with one click of a button, the whole lot were deleted. Gone.

I was unsubscribed from everything. I knew that any email that came into my environment would be something I had purposefully allowed to take my attention away, therefore must be important or add value to me. All my social media notifications were switched off so I could choose when I interacted with each platform, generally on the toilet. Come on, you all do it too.

I once again got that feeling of control, calm and being lighter. There weren't many left, but it also removed any lingering excuses not to try new things and new aspirations that had started to form. With all the experiences I had been through, a story was starting to build. It would have been wrong of me not to share and help others and, in some way, that would have to come out of me soon.

Every three months now I do a digital declutter. I remove any technology that simply doesn't add value and curate the timelines and accounts so I only interact with what I need. That constant tweak keeps it flexible and relevant. It also reduces my carbon footprint.

There was one more email I had to write, to the music venue where we hosted our Souterrain gigs. It was time to let that go too, and with that, I said goodbye to the final clutter from my previous life. It was time to start the next chapter. Never, in a million years, did I think I would end up where I am *now...*

19. Minimalist, Mostly

It's March 2020. Today, I am speaking at the Mindful Living Show in London, the largest mindfulness event of its kind in the UK. It's set up to support people to live healthier, happier lives with two days of learning, relaxation and mindfulness. These weird anniversaries are starting to become a thing as it's a year to the day, again, when I did my first talk at my friends' company. I've done dozens of talks over the last few months but this one is the biggest to date. It was still a little touch and go right up until a few days before due to the spread of coronavirus, but this event was still happening. My mug appeared alongside a line-up of renowned experts and pioneers in their field such as author and psychologist Rick Hanson and former model and animal rights activist Heather Mills. The previous year they had Ruby Wax and Russell Brand speak at their event. Hilariously, I'll be sharing a stage with a Buddhist monk, masters in sleep management, psychologists, yoga teachers, nutritional therapists and energy healers. Probably best if I keep the foul language to a minimum today then. One of India's great spiritual masters is on stage before me. I wonder if the curators had a laugh putting me on after someone so profound. "Let's stick this prick on afterwards to talk about donating his *Saved by the Bell* t-shirt shall we, and see what happens."

I quickly scan the room to see how the audience settles in. Some take out notebooks, others chat between themselves, a few sit quietly looking at me and the screen patiently waiting for this show to begin. It's this quick analysis of human behaviour and strangers together that allows me to choose how to begin.

"You will leave here with less," I say to the small crowd as they start to look quizzically at me and shuffle uncomfortably in their seats. I catch some smiles as I deliberately leave an awkward silence.

"I'm not a magician, nor a thief, but you will leave here with less than you came in with."

More chuckles sprinkle the room as I pace across the huge bright white screen with my name written in grey across the middle. Just after I commence, the door opens at the back of the room and dozens more people stroll through, trying to keep quiet whilst they search for space and empty chairs. Within a minute all available seats have been filled and the room is full. A handful of people stand at the back of the room.

My mouth all of a sudden becomes dry.

"Welcome to the discovery of less, an introduction to minimalism."

I survey the largeness of the room. The audience are listening.

"So, what can you expect from a talk by a minimalist...?' I begin as I walk to the left of the stage, gravitating towards the lectern, my safe haven. I've clocked a slight tear in the carpet right in front of the screen, one to keep an eye on as I could trip and fall on my face if I don't pay attention to it. As I click through to the next slide I pause to take in the moment; these strangers are here to listen to my story. And a story I shall give them.

Deep breath, here we go...

The importance of my life-changing decisions hit me when I was at a friend's house party just before Christmas 2018, a few weeks before my first ever talk on my take on minimalism. By then, I'd written a few blog posts about my experience of decluttering and how that leads into discovering the benefits of a minimalist lifestyle and published them on my website, lessisprogress.com, which I learnt how to make myself, another new skill to add to the collection. The feedback from my friends was positive as word had spread that Hayley and I had sold or donated virtually everything we owned, quit our jobs, went travelling, moved into a new home and that I'd changed career twice. People wanted to know more about this strange upheaval as well as stories from our adventures away.

It wasn't long before a barrage of questions came from all angles ranging from "Why did you sell everything?" to "Do you miss any of it?"

Because I was living my new lifestyle every day, I hadn't anticipated the impact it could have on others, so I began to share my story.

"At first I started to sell stuff in the flat for money so I could clear debt and pay for travelling. I then started to realise that the majority of stuff I had owned for so long actually owned me and no longer added value to my life. *The Karate Kid* boxset couldn't even help me pay for a diphtheria jab," I joked.

"That's because you didn't listen to Miyagi!" a friend quipped as the room roared with laughter.

"Once I started to see that selling or donating my belongings would actually help to move forward I worked my way through all of it and it turned out I hadn't used most of the things I had stored for so long. Stuff was just sitting there taking up room, distracting me and not giving anything back. In a way, all that old shit was just a manifestation, a representation, of a cluttered mind and the comfort zone I was living in. It kept me in a bubble of past mediocrity and busyness. I was stuffocated!

"Of course, selling the majority of the stuff then led to Hayley quitting her job and me taking a career break and then selling the flat to fund the rest of the trip."

My friends sat around the table transfixed. I could tell they had a million more questions.

"Then obviously we went travelling and visited ten countries – with each new country we realised we needed even less stuff to be content. Actually, the less stuff we had, the happier we were. When we returned, our bags were almost empty and my mind specifically was cleared of self-limiting thoughts; we both got new jobs, helped my mum and dad declutter, then I started to look at my digital life and decluttered there and realised how much junk I had on my phone that didn't add any value whatsoever. My social media was full of bullshit, so I just curated it all and made it work for me, connecting with people and topics that enhanced my experience of it. Oh, and the emails, the emails I had stored up was ridiculous.

"So all this stuff I removed just took a massive weight off my shoulders and it allowed me to focus forwards rather than being anchored in the same place doing the same things with the same stuff.

"So now I live a lot simpler, I feel lighter, my mind is less cluttered, I've got more money in my pocket and all the crap that I never used is now actually being used by someone else.

"Souterrain has gone as well. That's been wrapped up because it started to feel like a second job and stopped being fun. Ditching that has given me back my time, which I've used to set up Less is Progress website and tell these stories.

"I sold a load of my gear as well and it felt really good to let go of it, but I still like to buy things," Hayley added with a cheeky grin.

Her own minimalist journey had not gone as far as mine, she happily keeps control of her side of the wardrobe and that's enough for her. There are still regular parcels turning up at the flat for her, but she will check back in on her stuff a few times a year to make sure it's not got out of hand.

Twenty minutes went by in a flash and I'd retold true stories of letting go of physical possessions and the dangers of using language like 'one day', revealing terms like emotional clutter, commitment clutter, decision fatigue and analysis paralysis. It connected with them deeply as I recounted reactions to situations they'd also been in and real-life scenarios they could resonate with.

I paused for a moment and let my words sink in.

I'd just heard the brief re-telling of this story for the first time in a group setting.

The group all started to talk over themselves as they asked questions to their partners and I noticed the hosts started to look around their living room, surveying their material possessions that were just a few minutes ago part of the furniture, but now potentially in the way of something. They were processing new information and figuring out if the story had made them see things in a different way. People got animated; fingers started to get pointed in a jovial way. Ambitions and aspirations previously put to one side were rekindled and resurrected. It resonated and it sparked reaction. One friend declared they'd declutter their work van the following day because they generally spent ages looking for things, another announced that they felt motivated to go through a junk drawer and that's when I started to see the effect.

I got up from my seat as the crowd noise increased and headed towards the kitchen, picking up empty glasses along the way. I looked back at the living room, making sure I'd collected everyone's empties, and people were shuffling around the room swapping seats to sit next to others they wanted to chat with more intimately. Hayley was now answering questions from a smaller, more energetic trio that had broken away from the main group and gathered closer to her. As I moved further down the kitchen towards the freezer, the buzz of the living room started to diminish to a mere background muffle. I carefully lowered the glasses onto the counter and then opened the freezer in one swift movement. Just as the cold air hit me, I noticed a friend standing in the doorway between the chaos and noise of tipsy drinkers.

"Lovett, you should tell that story at events or something like that, it's inspirational! Do you want to speak at my company's HR event in a few weeks?" she proclaimed as I twisted an ice tray with just enough force to break a handful of cubes from the cells.

It was a thought that hadn't yet crossed my mind but as I stood there and listened to her relay stories of keynote speakers she'd previously hired for her own company, I started to see the appeal. It wasn't really something I'd ever done before and I noticed myself fidgeting and getting a little tense as I slowly poured out half a dozen rum and cokes, spilling a bit on the floor. The thought of being on stage, speaking in front of people about personal things, would be different. When I was on the radio, DJing in bars or introducing bands and artists on to a stage, I was playing a character or hiding behind the decks. It wasn't about me then, it was about the music, I was merely the facilitator. This time it would be me, up front, all alone on stage, vulnerable and sharing concepts, stories, advice and behaviours that I didn't yet feel were fully formed. The uncomfortable feeling I got was familiar now. Previously the sense of uncomfortableness would ring my risk-averse alarm bells and I'd go straight into excuse mode, layering up reasons why I couldn't, or shouldn't, do what was being proposed. It would have been safer to step backwards and become non-committal, remaining in my comfort zone. "Sure, one day, maybe," again came to mind. It was still a default option but if I waited to do things until I wasn't scared, I'd be waiting forever. I know now what is on the other side of a new, scary experiment. Growth, new experiences and another story to add to the collection. Letting go of the comfort zone time and time again over the last few years had led me to new and exciting things, so why stop now?

"Why the fuck not, right!" I responded, rejecting any previous hints of self-doubt.

The antidote to fear is action and I asked her to book me at her next event, which was in six weeks' time.

It's just telling stories in front of a bunch of strangers, I thought to myself, trying to digest what I'd just agreed to do as she walked out the room, hands in the air and announcing my first 'gig' as a speaker. I strolled in behind her with full glasses and carefully presented everyone with their replenished liquor as they all let up a cheer.

I claimed some space on the floor as my previous seat on the sofa was now taken and as I got comfortable Hayley gave me a smile from her new seated position across the room that cut through all the commotion and animation. I'd become accustomed to reading her facial expressions in social situations, she doesn't have to say a word and I can tell when she wants me to suggest leaving soon or get her a cup of tea or bring her into a conversation. I know it all and as she raised her eyebrows, I could read her expression once more and her face was saying, "That escalated quickly but you can practise on me!"

Time to level up, again. As well as a minimalist and a coach, I guess I'm a speaker now too. No pressure.

One of the Mindful Living Show event representatives raises a piece of large white card at the back of the room. On it a blue number five can be seen. That's my warning to start wrapping up. I'd delivered the core things that I wanted to get across, my story with some humour sprinkled in, some clutter stats and then a few simple tips that people could act on immediately.

"We've got a couple of minutes left, so does anyone have any questions?" I ask the audience.

The braver individuals are quick to put their hands up and share their own personal examples of clutter, and then ask me for advice. Each time, I throw the question back out to the audience and ask them what they would do, allowing them the opportunity to chip in and share even more advice collectively. I then give my answer as a way to bring that question to a resolve before inviting another question to be shared. This brings the audience together a bit more and they chat between themselves and openly disclose the excess within their environments. The community vibe within the group feels safe enough for them to share this information. The card at the back of the room is waved at me. Time to call it a day and I wrap it up.

"So, imagine a life with less ... less stress, less clutter, less cleaning, less debt. Now imagine a life with more ... more time, more ideas and more experiences. Thank you."

A ripple of generous applause cascades around the room. I smile and return back to the left of the screen, grabbing my bottle and downing half of my water, almost coughing it up.

Whilst most audience members get up with their belongings and leave the room, a dozen or so people come up to me afterwards and let me know their specific minimalist challenges. I love the talks, but this additional face-to-face question time is like an encore, and it's something that's starting to happen a lot more frequently. One specific person catches my eye in the crowd and she slowly makes her way over to me as I say goodbye to someone else. She shakes my hand and introduces herself to me.

"My friends call me the Bag Lady," she proudly announces.

She explains to me that people in her local community had given her that label due to her always carrying multiple bags of stuff around with her. It's something I had already noticed as she made her way into the room and found her seat. The Bag Lady is slight in frame but comes across as strong and confident. Her short haircut indicates a sense of precision and authority. I glance quickly down at her side to count the three large tote bags, two on her right shoulder and one on her left. Her default demeanour is to hold them tightly and close to her body like a safety blanket or something of high value.

Within a matter of minutes, the Bag Lady has become a focus of people's interest. We exchange pleasantries and although it is very much a conversation between the two of us, I am aware that a handful of people are starting to gather and listen intently as she shares her backstory. Her focus is on me, but the gathered throng hear the justifications for carrying the contents around every day shuffling to work, the shops and to her friends' houses. In a way to share her discomfort, she hands me the bags so I can feel the weight she is carrying around. I let out a cockney "Blimey!" as I lift them onto my shoulders for a brief moment before gratefully handing them back.

She explains that her back and shoulders are always hurting but it doesn't register that she has probably caused this pain herself.

Cosmetics, snacks, bottles, books, magazines, spare clothing and purses are just some of the items she retrieves and shows me. The purses, both slightly discoloured, are bursting at the seams with receipts and heavy with coins. Bottles of water are unfinished.

The bystanders shuffle in closer, unconsciously checking the weight of their own bags, awaiting the outcome of this conversation, expecting a magical piece of advice, but none is required.

This highly intelligent lady just talks to me and I see her going on her own journey, exploring how she arrived into this situation to discover that there was more long-term detriment that she had been blind to all along. The stuff that follows her around every day forged a new identity that was created for her. It costs her time (walks around slower), energy (used up quicker) and money (cloakroom, pain killers) and all these costs had been invisible until today.

Within this short window is an opportunity for her to reflect. A moment in time to just stop and see where the dots start to connect. It's not long before she starts to question everything that masquerades as important on her person, a mindset shift from a mere thirty minutes earlier.

"I don't want to be the Bag Lady anymore," she whispers to me as we embrace before she walks away back down the hall with a smile on her face. Her back straighter, chin higher.

As I shake the hand of the next person wanting to share, I feel obliged to just turn my head to see her one last time and catch a glimpse of her walking towards a nearby bin. She pauses for a moment and then starts to empty some of the bag's contents. One now empty bag gets folded up and placed into another.

Her bottles, once half empty, potentially now seem half full.

20. Discovery of Less

Yesterday.

I slept particularly well last night. Our new place is not too far distance wise from our previous home, but I am now "living" somewhere a lot further away. The physical surroundings are similar, but I live simpler, slower. I am living rather than existing. I am a human being rather than a human doing. Most things that are in my environment have been curated; we have one TV, a handful of books and minimal distractions in our living room. The kitchen is small but contains everything we need. We have more plants than plates. The bedroom is a mellow place of calm with no lamps, no alarm clock TV, no stress.

Our new rescue dog, Daisy, has been staring at me for about half an hour. Even though my eyes are closed, I can feel her less than a foot away. She knows that sitting and waiting by my face will eventually get me up and out of bed. She makes subtle movements on my side of the bed to make the smallest of noises in an attempt to stir me enough to give her attention. Daisy wakes up and starts to stretch just after sunrise as the glow of red creeps under the curtain on the floor; she'll maybe give it fifteen minutes before she wants something, so she is my alarm clock now. I reach my arm out to stroke her head and she nudges me towards the door. As I quietly remove the covers and sit up in bed, stretching, she is full of excitement, jumping up and down at the immediate prospect of food followed by a long walk around the quiet back streets of south London. She leaps towards the door and looks back at me to check I am following. While she has made progress in getting this human out of bed, she sprints back to my side whilst I pick out some adequate clothing for an hour's walk. Intently watching my every move, she tries to capture eye contact so she can hurry me along to the kitchen.

Imagine how long she'd have to wait if I still had all those clothes. Now I only have one small wardrobe of items, pretty much every item is hung up on individual hangers so I can see what's on offer. Gone are the days of two or three pairs of trousers on one hanger, creased and untidy together. All my clothes are my favourites, so it doesn't matter what I put on, I feel comfortable and content. Everything fits, I like them all and they are of good quality. I have a new rule that everything must be hung up, apart from underwear and socks of course, but I refuse to buy any more hangers. I've spent hours of my life untangling fucking hangers down the years, so I don't want any more. If a new piece of clothing comes in, a gift or a purchase, something has to go, so I intentionally haven't bought any new clothes for more than a year now. I can't tell you what's in or out of fashion.

Daisy is a bitsa. Bitsa this, bitsa that. Part Labrador, part Retriever, part Weimaraner. Hayley and I recently rescued her from the Dogs Trust. Daisy deserves a second chance away from a life being scared, malnourished and neglected. A tear in her right ear indicates a previous life of force and aggression and having to fight or defend. Her well-manicured jet-black fur is interrupted only by the greying around her loving eyes and chin indicating she is maybe nine or ten years old. Yes, she is a sweet old lady but when rubbed up the wrong way, I imagine she would talk like Catherine Tate's foul-mouthed nan, shouting over a fence and calling someone a mug.

While she scoffs away in her bowl hoovering up every single piece of her breakfast, I put my trainers on and grab my phone from the front room (it no longer follows me into the bedroom). There are more notifications than usual, so I open up my email to check the morning's subscriptions, which are now very few. One email reads:

"Great inspirational talk! Literally, the next day I started to declutter and made two surprisingly large piles of items to either sell or throw away. Thanks again for the inspiration!"

Another one reads, "Your talk gave me a lot to reflect on – thanks!"

Another reads, "I'm so looking forward to removing the chaos and stress of the clutter!"

The corners of my mouth turn up, wrinkling my eyes as they go back to the top of the email to make sure I've put all the words in the right order.

These are emails to keep. They remind me why I now do what I do.

Leaning up against the cold ceramic kitchen sink I peer outside the window at nothing in particular, content. Strangers have taken value from the talk, my talk, and have been positively impacted by my words and actions. Although it was never really planned that way, it totally connects to my values of influence and creative contribution and that works perfectly: the ability to help others through my story. There I find my fulfilment and sense of purpose. It gives me confirmation that I am on the right path, a new, scary and exciting path that I have curated. Hayley is my voice of reason and supports me with preparing the material and calling me a dickhead if I start to get too philosophical.

The road outside is quiet and the trees are starting to burst into spring life. Delicate yellows and reds are expressing themselves and the extra foliage is ample cover for the birds as they coo high up in their nests. Daisy's ferocious chomps into her bowl are fading away as background noise as I watch the leaves dance in rhythm with the light breeze. A subtle tap on the window brings my focus back as a bee loses its way and then flies off again into all the green.

The only thing I have to do right now is go for a nice relaxing stroll with Daisy before logging on for work. I find immense joy in seeing her tail wag as she sniffs around the freshly cut grass.

Daisy, full of excitement and the need for a toilet, bounds down the stairs towards the main road.

"Stay, Daisy," is a command she understands very well as we wait for the early morning traffic to disappear.

Walking is no longer just a means to an end; it is a thing on its own that I value greatly. Walking was the cheapest way to get from A to B but I now realise the bit in the middle is actually more important. No longer do I push forwards at pace, in a rush trying to get to the next place, or person, as quickly as possible. Now I take my time. I look up when walking, a shift from the 'head down and plough through' mentality. I stop and take pictures if I see something of interest. I've found new routes and paths to take that were there all along, but I'd never seen. My listening habits have changed since letting go of Souterrain. Some mornings I choose to learn, some mornings I want music, sometimes neither. Just silence. No longer am I driven by my own hustle to find the next amazing song or local artist before everyone else. Whatever I choose to listen to I do through intention, because it adds value. The notes section on my iPhone previously had lists of pointless purchases I wanted to make, I shit you not, it was actually called 'Shit I Need', but now they've been replaced by a ream of ideas, theories from thought leaders and questions I can ask myself and others. I now also see the different colours on the trees. Even if I get lost, I can always find my way back in the end. And actually, it's OK to get lost sometimes, it just adds to the story.

The lady who gets her paper in the morning from the local shop gives me a wave every day, I smile and wave back. The old couple who walk their dog Lola stop and chat with me from across a quiet road and ask how Daisy is getting on. We keep our distance, so Daisy doesn't get scared by the other dog. The guy who lives in the block of flats next door walks his dog and nods at me; one of us always crosses the road to avoid any barky conflict or excitement between the two pooches. There's the dude who strolls around with two new-borns in their pram, he raises a hand at me while he listens to his music. The lady who runs each morning with her sunglasses on and huge headphones smiles and raises her hand to wave as she jogs past. I stop and spare a minute or two with the lollipop lady who makes sure the kids and parents are crossing the road to the school safely. She's not hard to spot in her high vis but she is out there every school day, come rain or shine, and she's very popular. She remembers everyone's names. All these interactions with strangers are brief but they play a small part in building a positive platform for the day ahead.

In between waving and nattering with the locals and stopping Daisy from eating dog shit, the walk gives me ample opportunity to reflect on my contribution to my peers over the last few days it also allows me to question what I've learnt, what I've discovered and how I've bettered myself from the previous day. With having less stuff to do, I am clearer on what needs to be done, what I can accomplish, and where I can break things in order to make them better.

I get Daisy home and she saunters up the steps and waits for me to open the front door to our flat; she pushes her nose so close to the door so she can be the first one in. Once let back in she checks to see if there's any food left and once she has explored the area, she grabs a drink from her bowl. I will start work soon but there is always time for a bit of roughhousing with Daisy before she has another nap. She's clearly living her best life.

I tend to work from home much more now. My new 'nine to five' coaching job is flexible and works for me. I combine having a corporate job that aligns to my motivations and values with continuing to contribute to society by creating meaningful talks, articles and tools as well as coaching and mentoring others to unlock their potential by ditching their stuff. It's my version of a successful minimalist lifestyle. I figured out the other day that I had listened to over 15,000 minutes of podcasts on walks over the past year, about 250 hours. That's a bit mad. In that time, however, I've discovered what my version of a minimalist lifestyle looks and feels like and I also know what I have no interest in. I have little to no interest in minimalist architecture or racing to see who has the least number of things. I'm sure others get great value out of keeping tabs, but it just doesn't work for me. I don't want to obsess over counting my stuff. I also get why some people would wear or gravitate to the same white or black colours all the time, it's simple and that's their version of a minimalist life, but I still like to throw some colours and logos on now and then. I feel like I've spent enough time in my own black and white story, it's time to live in a world of colour. In crafting this lifestyle, I've learnt that having a minimalist mindset is only a tool, it's not an outcome.

From the old DVDs I no longer watched to the clothes I hardly wore, the furniture that didn't add value, the instruments I ignored. The bits, the pieces, the attachments to things I no longer owned. The things we didn't need existing with stuff that was no longer loved. The home that had all my things I thought was complete, however without those things I am already complete. I've now started a collection of experiences outside of the norm; travel was the greatest investment in self-development and growth I could ever have wished for. Just as valuable as any course you would go on. I have even added it to my CV.

The return on investment in stopping, for just a moment, was far greater than the need to keep going.

From the physical to the digital, the habits, questions, challenges and feelings from jettisoning the stuff I could touch helped in cleansing my digital footprint. No longer distracted by pings and bleeps, whatever I let into my environment is there by necessity. I bring it in because there is value in it. How is this thing going to positively impact me or the people around me?

The mental clutter and the stories I told myself played their part in keeping me at just the right level of safe. I can now be more aware when these stories come up and let them go if they don't benefit me.

My new minimalist lifestyle and mindset has unlocked my potential to craft a career that aligns with who I want to be and how I show up every day. It's removed all the self-made boundaries and glass ceilings. It's helped me contribute significantly to the betterment of individuals, teams, families and communities, something I knew I could do but never knew how. This lifestyle has unlocked an increased level of courage, resilience and bravery to try and create new things. All these life experiences, successes and achievements were there all along, but I was consumed by the stuff I'd surrounded myself with. Now I live with less. Less physical, digital and mental clutter, less debt, less self-sabotaging, less stress.

On the flipside, I also now live with more. More time, more ideas, more creativity, more confidence, more self-awareness, more control, more knowledge and actually more money.

When I discovered less, I found so much more.

Epilogue

*"Day one or one day,
you decide."*
Paulo Coelho

This is only the beginning...

My journey into discovering less doesn't end at the conclusion of the final chapter, in fact I don't think it will ever really end. This lifestyle and mindset is just a tool to help bulldoze stuff out of the way and in doing so enhance the chances of achieving the things you want to. However, if you don't know your 'why' yet, that's OK, generally things become clearer when you can see a way forward.

Hayley has changed jobs twice as well recently, not settling for workplace cultures and politics that she didn't feel comfortable in, and I loved those decisions that she made. If she felt something was off, she did something about it. She no longer gets held hostage by a job, and whether she knows it or not, she is an inspiration to me and a role model for those she works with now.

My folks have started to embrace decluttering as well, if only a little bit more than when I left them with it last time. There are more questions now that they ask of each other, such as "What are we going to do with (the thing)?" which is a great place to start. I was so proud of my mum when she decided to let go of a bag of stamps that were from my nan's house, her mum, after she passed away. There were hundreds of them in a plastic bag ranging from commemorative royal first-class ones to historic world or sporting anniversaries. They weren't collectables or anything, just freebies you get in magazines or with newspapers. My mum had no use for them, but she just could not detach herself away from the sentiment that they were her mum's things, so they had to stay in their home and have some use. There they sat, in a plastic bag in the hallway for weeks, until one day she came to me and asked for some help selling them. It was then she realised that some-body else would be better off with the stamps. I kept her abreast of how much each batch sold for, which was generally only a few quid, and they were soon all bought up by a few individuals who wanted them. I went to the cashpoint and withdrew the money after all the PayPal transactions went through (she still likes cash over electronic payments) and she could hold the thirty-odd quid and a few coins in her hands, which she put towards a new cake stand that she had wanted for a while.

My mum has also benefitted from my dad's little online record shop that he has going. Although my dad and I work together on selling his unwanted records, he gets all the money from any sales. Looking back, I probably should have negotiated a brokerage fee or something, that was an opportunity missed! I do the sales bit up front alongside the techy stuff, like adding his records to the Discogs website and communicating via email with any prospective buyers. He is still finding boxes of vinyls under the stairs, in boxes in the loft and in suitcases in the garage from his mum and dad's when they passed away. I arrange all the payments through PayPal and give him the cash as like my mum, he doesn't like electronic payments and prefers holding notes in his hand and having coins in his pockets. When an order comes through online, I get an email, so I tell him which ones have sold and where they need to be posted to. Dad then finds the record from boxes stacked up in the study or in my brother's old bedroom and walks to the post office to send them off. His collection of records added to the site is currently at 1,850. That's not all of them. He set a bar early that any that were valued over £10 and that he was happy to part with, would be put up for sale, so that number stands at 519. There are still a few he doesn't want to let go of such as any Steely Dan record and anything by Toto or Chicago. From the LPs and singles he has put up for sale, 182 have sold over the last three years, which equates to just over £5,000. £5,000 that was just sitting in his loft. Madness.

My folks are fully retired now but they are still full of energy, they travel more than Hayley and I do. Every couple of months they're in some part of the UK with friends visiting places they've not been to before. My dad has bought a new lawnmower with his record money, they go out for dinner, they've redecorated the kitchen, all sorts. Funded by crap they never used or even realised was there.

They are, however, still dealing with the excess stuff from my grandparents' homes and that still takes up room in their living spaces, so it makes you think about the things we leave behind for our loved ones: where is the line between passing down heirlooms and memories to leaving responsibilities behind for others to deal with?

"One day, son, this will all be yours," Dad says to me.

Oh, bollocks.

I've made significant financial investments in myself as well recently, becoming a multi-disciplined coach, so I can now support even more people with even more skill and expertise in their life and career. When I was pivoting my career, I couldn't find many people to talk to who had done the same. They could only offer advice within a certain industry or discipline that they knew, which wasn't broad enough, so I went and became a career coach as well. I've been spending more time with really interesting coaches and thought leaders to further my own abilities and awareness. My teachers, supervisors and friends, Sonya and Lucy from Ride The Wave Coaching (check them out), are inspirations, not only because they are shit hot at what they do, but also because they have social impact and fun at the heart of everything they do, which aligns well with my own values and aspirations. I've also had the opportunity to support others who I respect massively with their own book projects. Jeff Weigh and his project *Stuck! Now What?* and Andy Storch and his book *Own Your Career Own Your Life* are well worth checking out.

Because of all this learning, listening and increased awareness and championing of self and others, I've seen first-hand how saying "no" has become a important skill. People pleasers, beware. I've coached highly skilled, highly intelligent and incredibly well-paid individuals out of disastrous holes that they have found themselves in by saying "yes" all the time and not wanting to let others down. Or, wanting to be seen as the most important motherfucker in the virtual room. The realisation that you've taken on too much hits you long after you agree to it all, so the ability to know your own capacity, make time for yourself and challenge back on what the priorities are, will need to be levelled up; otherwise in the long run, no one wins.

I've seen big clients walk away from small businesses and the near collapse of a start-up caused by people overworking, fixing other people's problems (not letting them find out the answer for themselves) and then burning out, just because that little bit of help would only take a few minutes to sort. The ability to prevent things stacking up, physically and metaphorically, is now vital to how we progress through life. You don't want to be looking back at a load of hoarded crap or a team in your organisation so exhausted from putting more on their plate and then thinking, "How did we get into this mess?"

Piles of yes all over the shop.

Since the final words of this book were written, the country has gone into several lockdowns over the coronavirus pandemic. Although I decluttered my intake of news, there were things that I saw that displayed how the habits and behaviours of society came through in times of crisis. Looking outside my kitchen window I would see consumers cradling countless rolls of toilet paper. The news would display images of ransacked supermarket shelves and a significant rise in people's desire for penne pasta. I was amazed that the priority was the cleanliness of the rear end and cooking a pasta bake, but I was also not surprised that we, as a group of people, reacted by hoarding a load of stuff. Seeing others panic-buying generated a sense of urgency, so everyone did it. Cars were being loaded up to the brim with enough food to feed an army and all this made people feel a little more secure, maybe even a little more in control in a situation that was bordering out of it. It's not only a time of uncertainty but also a period in which many of us could be experiencing social isolation, which may motivate us to buy stuff we don't need. In fact, total retail sales in September 2020 were over 5 per cent higher than pre-Covid levels in February, according to the Office of National Statistics.

In a weird way, what the pandemic offered was another

forced opportunity for people to really take stock of the things they had inside their homes as well as what was going on in their lives. Stuck indoors for excessive amounts of time was the exact moment where we could use all of those 'just in case' items such as all the books we never had time to read and play the board games we insisted on keeping but never used. Being in quarantine elevated the need for human contact and we reached out to people who maybe we hadn't spoken to for a while, to check in on them. We reconnected with people and the desire to support our communities was elevated, but did we reconnect with the stuff that had been part of our environment for so many years? Maybe some of us did, maybe some of us didn't. In that time, we saw an estimated sixty-seven million items of clothing and twenty-two million pairs of shoes donated to charity shops according to the government-backed recycling body, Wrap, with two in five of us having a wardrobe clear-out during the pandemic. However, the UK now makes up 41 per cent of the European self-storage market and has the most storage per person of any country in Europe. I get that they can be a great temporary thing, but I guess each person's view on how long temporary actually is, can vary.

We were all forced to stop in our tracks and in doing so it gave an opportunity for us all to understand what was truly important. So, what's important to you now?

Previous events would have jolted some people to question their purchasing habits and physical, digital, mental and emotional clutter. The credit crunch of 2008 forced a different approach to spending. You could say it also birthed the westernised and more modern minimalism lifestyle. For a time, the 'sparking joy' trend of Marie Kondo pushed Netflix subscribers to see magic in tidying up. A generation hit by recession has caused a rise of tiny homes, having to make do with less and amplified by more mainstream shows such as *Tiny House Nation*. The one negative trigger event often required to shake us out of our bubble has now impacted pretty much all of us. We've all experienced significant disruption, some more so than others, but it's a wake-up call to question the need for relentlessly going through To-Do lists, compromising time with loved ones and spending money we don't have in bad places on shit we don't really need to impress people we don't really like.

Millions of families are a month's pay away from falling into arrears on household bills, so if the rug was to suddenly be pulled out from under your feet, what would you do? Now could be the best time to understand what your values are and get clear on the things that enhance your life from the shit that just gets in the way.

As for me, well I'm not exactly sure how many items I own now – I'm not that bothered with counting or sticking to rigid frameworks, you've probably worked that out by now – but I do try to not bring too much into my environment because the likelihood is, I'll only have to deal with it further down the line. I even received an Amazon gift card for my birthday this year and it took me months to work out what I wanted to buy. Eventually I bought some books and a replacement iPhone battery but I'm sure there is still a few quid left on it. Speaking of Amazon, I stumbled on this new quirk that I had been blind to before. Yes, my purchasing habits have significantly reduced, I've spent more money on experiences like gigs, shows (obviously reduced in 2020-21) and large Cadburys Easter Eggs than on physical items, but I noticed that when I had a shot of consumeristic energy, I would search for something online and then consciously leave it in the basket. This happened a few times, most recently with a card game of some sort, like Cards Against Humanity but newer. I spotted this when I was getting someone else a secret Santa gift and, once again, thought I'd treat myself. This time, the cards stayed in the basket and I forgot about them. They clearly weren't that important otherwise I would have remembered to buy them the following day, week or month. There they sat, waiting and waiting, and by the next time I logged back into Amazon to buy Daisy some dog food, that desire for those cards had gone and I removed them from my cart.

So, there's something to think about.

I've written a lot about removing stuff but being able to not just then replace the stuff you've discarded with more stuff is also really important. If you're able to leave something in your virtual basket for a few days and then forget about them, it may be that the thing you were about to buy was never that important anyway. And, of course, if it is, you'll go back when you're ready and order as normal.

I gave my PlayStation 3 to my brother and I'm quick to donate any clothes that no longer fit or get used. My time spent packing has reduced massively. There was a wedding last year that Hayley and I were invited to, which would generally have meant me spending ages trying on things and picking the best outfit. Bits of clothes and accessories left all over the floor, stress, panic and loads of decision fatigue. However, this time, it took me twenty minutes to pick which suit I was going to wear (because I only have a small choice now and they're all quality) plus what accessories, tie, shirt and shoes were going to go with it. It was all ironed, bagged up and ready to go. That was a milestone hit.

The next time we pick up and either move home or go travelling again, I can quite happily detach myself from the majority of the few material possessions that enhance our home. I'm not precious about the sofa or the chest of (Chester) drawers. The tables we bought from eBay can happily go back on there and be used by someone else. I'm willing to let go of the bricks and mortar and sell it off in exchange for creating more experiences. In fact, by the time you read this we'll have definitely moved again.

I don't really have a five-year plan, but I see travelling in our future again at some point, whether that's being more UK based and becoming more digital nomady and shifting around every six months, I'm not sure, but we've got the bug. I see more speaking and more listening taking place as the message of less starts to become ever more popular. I want to be the best coach I can be so I can help others unlock their potential, so more learning and connecting with fascinating people will also happen. That's exciting. Eventually, I'll dip out of the corporate world when the time is right, but at this moment, I've crafted fulfilment and flexibility from my job to also pursue writing, telling stories and coaching on the side. But it's not really on the side, it's on the same plate, like a healthy serving of veg.

Although at times writing this book was an absolute ball-ache, on the whole I really enjoyed this project. I lost about 7,000 words somewhere, who the fuck knows where they went. I remember spending a few days writing and re-writing the first chapter and then switching on the laptop one day to find that it had magically disappeared. I'd written the word 'declutter' so much that the book started to declutter itself! I did learn where my limits were though when I started to look back on the previous day's words and delete pages and pages of absolute tosh, so I got really disciplined in writing only when I was near or in a flow state, mostly in the mornings. When the words didn't come, it was best to stop and go again the following day, otherwise I just wasted time and energy. It was tough sometimes to shut the lid when I was really trying to finish a paragraph or replace a sentence, but that ability to stop has made me enjoy the process more and I can actually see me doing a few more of these in the future.

There's another 13,000 or so words that were cut from this final version so they may appear in other pieces on the blog, so you can head over to lessisprogress.com and read some other bits and pieces. I also believe there's a book in all of us. We've all got a story to tell.

There is also the '30 Days of Less' e-book on there you can download too, obviously I recommend it. It's the shit. I created that after seeing a lot of questions from people on social media and other communities asking where to start their journey of less. Sometimes, just starting anything new can be so overwhelming that we never actually start at all, so to give people a leg up, I made this easy-to-use guide which focuses on five areas over a month to dig into: digital space, career and work life (not as in ditching your job but reducing the wasted effort, although ditching your job is also an option), your living space, mental clutter and commitment clutter. I didn't really know what I was doing when I started my journey, so I started with proximity. My entertainment was the closest thing that I could see and touch on that day, however you may wish to start somewhere with less emotion attached, like the 3D glasses you kept from the cinema because you'd use them again when you next went, but actually never did. Plus, if you're goal orientated, each thing you detach yourself from is like a win and each win builds momentum, good form and motivation. Like beating the boss on a video game at the end of level one, the next-level bad guy is ready for you. Letting go of even one thing each day for a month sets you up nicely for a great hot streak. We deserve a hot streak. You deserve a hot streak. Less is progress, remember.

So, the only thing left for you to do now is close this book, take a deep breath and, when you're ready, let's cut the crap.

Glossary

Page 16, Declut – My weird saying when it's time to declutter. One less syllable.

Page 13, Less is Progress – My website and saying. I believe that when we focus on less, we achieve so much more. Therefore, less is progress, whatever progress looks like to you.

Page 13, Mental Desktop – Like your computer desktop with short cuts and things, just in your head.

Page 10, I had to reset – I always remember this little white reset button on my Sega Megadrive when I was younger. Whenever I got livid at my inability to get past the end boss on level seventeen of *Decap Attack* or fall into a spiral of debt on *Theme Park*, I would get up from the floor and aggressively hold it down, making the picture on the TV go all fuzzy before going black and slowly returning to the Sega start-up screen. Any activity that went on before it was eliminated immediately, and I got to try again, if I had the patience. What does your reset button look like?

Page 14, Minimalist Mindset – The approach of always questioning whether the task, thing, potential purchase or choice is really adding value. It's taking decluttering material possessions into all areas of life, not just your home.

Page 23, Pengest Munch – This is a very niche reference but there was this young guy called Elijah Quashie who became a very brief YouTube sensation because he critiqued London fried chicken shops. His reviews are hilarious and well crafted. Go check him out.

Page 26, Pub Golf – It's not golf. It's just pubs and lots of drinking. Wearing golf attire is encouraged. You may actually drop a shot if you aren't wearing ridiculous trousers or have a tee behind your ear. FORE!

Page 14, Conscious Uncoupling – Deliberate act of extracting myself away from things or extracting things from my environment.

Page 49, Known Unknown – Walking towards something you have no idea about to help unlock connections in your mind so a new idea can materialise, creating an opportunity that was never there before.

Page 54, Plates to spin, balls to juggle – A circus act that features as a metaphor for doing too many things, being over-busy or multi-tasking. I came up with the line "multi-tasking is not a skill, it's a risk" the day after I tried to make a nice roast dinner for Hayley and me. The oven was beeping indicating that the chicken was done, I was mashing potato, the veg was boiling, the gravy needed whisking and of course as I was balancing all the pots, pans, plates and drinks, I dropped the mashed potato on the kitchen floor. Oh, also I set the smoke alarm off as well, so I was also trying to turn that off by waving my tea towel in the air. There were too many things going on, so inevitably, I found dog hair in the mash. The rest of it was good though.

Page 57, Shoulding All Over Myself – Like shitting everywhere, but shoulding. I should do this, I should do that, I should complete this. It's a mindset that we get in where we convince ourselves that we need to do more. When we stop and think, we probably need to just change 'should' to 'could' and remove any pressure it causes. Once it becomes 'could' it's then a choice, not an obligation we've forced on ourselves.

Page 72, Self-Coaching – As a qualified coach, I feel that with an increased awareness of self, I can elevate away from the pressures of life and start to declutter my mind, I ask myself questions, like a coach would, to get to the root of the mental clutter.

Page 61, Shoppers High – A dopamine hit in the brain. The neurotransmitter surges when we are about to buy something new. It's a similar rush to drinking and gambling.

Page 72, Endowment Effect – In psychology it's the understanding that people are more likely to retain something they own than acquire the same thing that is not owned by them. Basically, we increase the value of something just because we own it, regardless of actual value. It's why people generally want to set their house price higher because it's theirs. There is an interesting study by Ziv Carmon and Dan Ariely on this topic relating to the price of NCAA tournament tickets, go check it out.

Page 151, Give me the hump – Aggressive annoyance. I actually say it without an 'H', feels better that way. "Got the 'ump'".

Page 160, 175, False Stories – You don't have to believe every stupid thing you think.

Page 190, Digital MOT – Ministry of Transport test. The annual check on the car to test its roadworthiness and safety. Doing something similar for your digital and actual body and mind roadworthiness might be a good addition.

Page 198, Diphtheria jab – That was one of the injections we had to get prior to going to certain countries in Asia. I was in and out of the doctors every week for about two months ticking off their list of recommended jabs.

Page 199, Stuffocated – Suffocated with STUFF!

Page 205, Human Doing – Timothy Gallwey writes in *The Inner Game of Tennis* that players who perform best aren't really doing at all, they're being. They're not over-thinking, they're merely present.

Page 209, Roughhousing with Daisy – She thinks our bed is now her bed, so she'll jump on there after her morning walk and wants to play. She indicates play by putting her butt in the air for us to scratch. She certainly does shake it like a Polaroid picture.

Page 215, Piles of Yes – A build-up of all the things you have said yes to. It's a backlog of tasks or commitments you have signed up to complete or others have given you.

Work
With Chris

LESS IS PROGRESS

So, what's next?

It's one of my go to questions with coaching clients. What would you like to do next? If you've come this far, you've hopefully finished the book, which is a pretty impressive achievement in itself, so good job!

"Can I get an encore, do you want more?" – Jay-Z

30 Days of Less eBook (or FreeBook)

"I'm so overwhelmed, I just don't know where to start"

I mentioned the 30 Days of Less eBook earlier, if you're feeling motivated and ready to start simplifying, you can subscribe to lessisprogress.com and you'll get it free. That will give you 30 areas to focus on to kick start and disrupt your physical, digital and mental clutter, plus your commitment and career stuff that is getting in the way of you being you 2.0. Crack on at the start of a month (30 days, 30 areas – see what I did there) or whenever you like.

If you'd like to work with me in real life, then these workshop and mentoring sessions could be for you. All booking and FAQ stuff on lessisprogress.com...

Simplicity Coaching & Mentoring

If you would like some 1:1 support then I'd love to be your cheer-leader as you declutter your life, simplify your work, change careers or just live better with less. I am an accredited executive, leadership, career, team and life coach. I'm also a qualified football coach but you probably don't need that bit. If you're ready to develop your own minimalist mindset, let go of your stuff and redesign your life to be better and do better, with less, then this could be for you.

You know me, you know my story, now let's create one for you.

Speaking & Group Workshops

I can talk a good game too! I'm a bit different. I'm one of the UK's only speakers to come and talk to groups and organisations about doing LESS! I share the psychology behind letting go, why we get caught up in busyness and teach you a few techniques on how to start ditching your personal and professional stuff. The world has changed and the traditional approach to life and work needs to evolve. It's disruptive, it's progressive and it's likely something your team, department or organisation needs right now.
All bookings are available on lessisprogress.com

But don't just take my word for it...

"Great inspirational Talk! Literally the next day I started to declutter and made two surprisingly large piles of items to sell or donate. It's really made a difference - we feel a little less claustrophobic. Thanks again for the inspiration."
Nick G

"We really enjoyed your story and the experiences you brought resonated with many of us, encouraging us to think beyond the extra "stuff" we own and also question what is stopping us from letting go of it. Your open and relatable approach ensured the session was relaxing and interactive. It really helped me think about decluttering both physical items but also in other aspects of my professional life."
Lisa W

"Prior to chatting with you, I was feeling unmotivated and 'stuck'. You challenged my perspectives and I was encouraged to critically reflect, which was both challenging and rewarding. You helped me realise that I can take control of my environment and not just

let stuff happen to me. I left feeling empowered to make positive changes, which I have now done. Thank you so much."
Ilijana P

"My new work approach is so simple, I had the answers all along but I was just so caught up people pleasing that I had no time to think for myself. All of a sudden I've got some time back. It's crazy to think I just got used to living at 100mph doing things that on reflection didn't make much difference to anyone."
Michelle T

"I've been fortunate to receive coaching from Chris on several occasions. I have access to numerous coaches and I specifically chose Chris as I find him hugely professional and trustworthy. I found his style really supportive and calming."
Sarah S

"It felt such a calming place to be and so refreshing given my work is mostly chaos."
Katherine N

"It was really useful and refreshing knowing others feel the same about their stuff. I picked up on some good ideas to help me deal with some of the ways in which I can work more efficiently and also more importantly, what I need to say to others around me, including my boss. I just wanted to say thank you, I feel a lot better after your session."
Felicity N

"Thank you so much for today's session, really inspiring. You gave me so much confidence!"
Hardev J

"Thank you so much for everything you did, it really has genuinely helped with my email maintenance and managing of self."
Georgie D

"I'd been wanting to leave my current employer for a while but always found justification in putting it off. Chris was the catalyst that gave me confidence and self-belief to start my new career."
Tom D

So, what's next for you?

LESS IS PROGRESS

Acknowledgements

Big up!

Right, let's get real for a minute. There are a lot of people that have inspired me to be who I am today, and encouraged me to continue to break things and think differently, and supported me in my personal and professional life, as well as those who put so much time and effort into helping me put this whole thing together. If you didn't make this list, you've been decluttered! Na, I'd love to thank everyone that has somehow played a role in me getting to do this stage but my editor would lose his shit so I'm keeping it as concise as possible.

So, here goes… a huge love and thanks to….

Hayley, bless her, who has been so patient and supportive with me sitting on the sofa in our old flat and wandering off into the spare bedroom / home office to tap away on random sentences and thoughts. She has been more than a legend in adventuring with me and allowing me to use her as a soundboard, even when she was in the middle of watching *Downton*. "What do you think about…" or "How does this sound…" were my regular interruptions.

I can't thank Hayley without thanking our dog Daisy, too. Her waking me up with old lady huffs every morning has forced me to go for long walks and embrace learning as well as becoming a master shit picker upper. I'm afraid those services are not for hire though.

My Mum and Dad, Rose and Ian, for letting me document part of their own decluttering journey and for letting Hayley and I crash at theirs for a few months post-travelling. Homemade cake, cookies and savouries everyday for six months! We've not been the same weight since.

My brother Gary, a pwopa geezer who fixes the things that I can't fix and helped clear out every place I've lived so I suppose he knows how to declutter properly now.

My editor, Malcolm Croft, and designer, Matt Windsor, for being absolute superstars and guiding me through what a real book should look, sound and feel like. Without their input, energy and belief, this would have been a fucking mess, maybe. We did this all virtually, across two continents in a global pandemic, yo!

My mates in the sausage club whatsapp group and #1 international beer pong squad, MT, Birdy, Lukey, Gareth and JP who will forever be the ones that inadvertently pushed me to get started by trying to convince me to download Mario Kart on my phone. I had to tell them no that day, because I was writing a book about minimalism. They promptly replied "A book about minimalism, surely that's just chapter 1 - get rid of your shit. Chapter 2 - have you got rid of it yet? Done" Thanks chaps x

Carley Dale – for being the catalyst and pushing me to talk at your companies away day. Without your encouragement and support, the rest of them may not have happened!

The Babies & Banter Brigade for all the love and meme Fridays. THE BEST interruption to writing.

Much love to the early readers who volunteered their time to play a pivotal role in getting this book out there, catching last minute typos and errors as well as providing thoughtful and constructive feedback.

A huge thanks to my peoples – this ragtag bunch who have now become pivotal in helping me believe, mentored me, coached me, checked in, pushed me out of my comfort zone, connected me with others, accepted my different ways of thinking and became a hugely influential part of my life. I'm just gutted it took me so long to find you all. Jeff Weigh, Garry Turner, Olga Piehler, Lucy Mullins, Sonya Shellard, Mark Elliott, Rich Cooper, Becky Gulliver, Jason Kelly, Andy Duncan, Fran Niedt, Sarah Skelton, Mahji Quadir, Kat Hutchings and Chris Senior.

If you haven't got a group of diverse people around you to learn from, listen to, speak openly with and use as a soundboard, go build yourself one.

There are of course, those who have influenced me that you probably saw in the book. I've spent considerable time listening and absorbing words from Josh & Ryan (The Minimalists), Joshua Becker, Courtney Carver, Colin Wright, Greg McKeown, Cait Flanders, Andy Storch, TK Coleman, Seth Godin, Whitney Johnson, Jason Fried and Jamil Qureshi and many others.

I couldn't write a book without dropping a big thanks to those previous leaders who gave this big haired, graffiti jacket wearer and authentic disruptor a chance. UJ who is 'Amanda' is the pick of the bunch but there have been a handful of other superstar leaders, who empowered me to be creative, bin off a load of stuff and challenge the traditional ways of thinking. You know who you are.

My old team at the green heart place – we all went off and did good. You're all legends.

I've got so much time for the people who took their time to provide endorsements, support me and this book, invite me on their podcasts, connect me into book clubs, write testimonials and allow me virtually into their living spaces to share good conversation. Bruce Daisley, Lisa J Shultz, El Deane, Justin Malik, Andy Cope (again), Caroline Rogers, Amy Revell, Kirsty Farrugia, Gav Thompson, Tania Diggory, James Warwick, Ebony, Ryan, Ingrid, Gail, Robert – thank you.

Acknowledgements

Colleagues and clients, past and present, thank you for trusting me with your challenges, personal and professional, sharing successes, exploring your purpose, identifying your blockers and figuring it all out.

A final thanks to you, the reader. Wherever you are, whatever you're doing, I hope you enjoyed this story and if any of it has inspired you into action, please share with me at **info@lessisprogress.com** or via the socials. Let's all hear your story.

To keep up to date with Less is Progress and connect with me, you can:

Check out the Facebook Page:
www.facebook.com/LessisProgress

Follow bitesize thoughts on Twitter:
www.twitter.com/ChristoLovett

See what I see and follow my slow travels on Instagram:
www.instagram.com/christolovett

Read the blog, use free resources plus get occasional stories and discounts on services on Less is Progress:
www.lessisprogress.com

Support my work by tipping me or my dog,Daisy, a biscuit. If you buy one and say it's for her, I take a short slow mo film of her trying to catch it and tag you in it. That in itself is a treat:
www.buymeacoffee.com/chrislovett

ISBN   978-1-8384375-0-3

Made in the USA
Monee, IL
31 January 2022